Chronicle

Fascinating People and Memorable Events of 1996

97

HAPPY BIRTHDAY MR. PRESIDENT

Chronicle 97
Written, edited, and designed by

Grant Laing Shane
Editorial and Design
Garden Studios, 11-15 Betterton Street,
London WC2H 9BP

A DK Publishing Book

GLS EDITORIAL AND DESIGN

Project editor Victoria Sorzano
Design director Ruth Shane
Editorial directors Reg Grant, Jane Laing

Author Reg Grant
Contributors Victoria Sorzano, Adrian Gilbert, Jane Laing

Picture research David Towersey, Frances Vargo
Index Kay Ollerenshaw

DORLING KINDERSLEY

Project editor Annabel Morgan
US editor Mary Sutherland
Production manager Ian Paton

Managing art editor Derek Coombes
Managing editor Frank Ritter

First published in the United States in 1996
by DK Publishing, Inc.
95 Madison Avenue, New York, NY 10016

A catalog record is available from the Library of Congress
ISBN 0-7894-1396-5

Reproduced by Kestrel Digital Colour Ltd., Chelmsford, Essex, UK
Printed and bound in the United States by R.R. Donnelley & Sons

Chronicle

97

Fascinating People and Memorable Events of 1996

Highlights of the year 1996

Shannon Lucid receives a call from the president after her record stay in space.

Theodore Kaczynski is arrested, suspected of being the long-sought Unabomber.

US gymnast Kerri Strug completes her vault despite an ankle injury at the Atlanta Olympics.

New York Yankees' John Wetteland is mobbed as his team wins the World Series.

WHAT WILL WE ALL remember of the year 1996? It was a year of tragedy—events such as the TWA 800 and Valujet crashes, the death of Commerce Secretary Ron Brown, and the terrorist bombing at Dhahran, Saudi Arabia. Terrorism even struck the Centennial Olympics in Atlanta. But 1996 was even more a year of courage—the courage of actor Christopher Reeve fighting paralysis and Muhammad Ali fighting Parkinson's disease, the courage of Olympic gymnast Kerri Strug and of record-breaking astronaut Shannon Lucid. The brave example of these individuals touched the heart of America.

Grozny, the Chechen capital, was devastated by Russian firepower.

The West African state of Liberia was racked by civil war.

Violence returned to the scarred streets of Northern Ireland.

Israeli security forces confronted rioting Palestinians in Jerusalem.

Airman Dwayne Dumas gives the thumbs up after surviving the Dhahran truck bombing that killed 19 US servicemen.

A grief-stricken Alma Brown is comforted by the president at her husband's funeral.

Russian president Boris Yeltsin dances his way to reelection in his country's first fully free elections. His victory was soon undermined by serious health problems.

The race for the White House

ALL OBSERVERS AGREE that this was not a presidential election year that set the US on fire. The turnout of under 50 percent of voters told its own story. Americans like a race with many dramatic twists, and one that goes to the wire. This was not it. President Bill Clinton led in the opinion polls from the start of the year and, riding the wave of a buoyant economy, never really looked like he was going to lose.

Hot contest

The battle for the Republican nomination was probably the hottest phase of the political year. Once the backers of Steve Forbes and Pat Buchanan lost the Republican debate to the cautious Bob Dole, politics was squeezed into the center ground. ʹ

At the start of the year Republicans had hopes that the Whitewater case and "Filegate" might sink the White House in scandal. But, despite a steady trickle of revelations, little of the dirt stuck. A last-minute scandal about possibly illegal foreign contributions to the Clinton campaign fund came far too late to have much effect.

Campaign winner

Republicans complained that the president stole their ideas and their policies. But responding to clear messages from a conservative, security-conscious electorate was a ploy that worked for Clinton. He slashed welfare, took credit for budget cuts, got tough on crime, and adopted the family as the focus of his campaign. Bob Dole was left pushing a 15 percent cut in income tax as his sole big policy.

As a campaigner, Bob Dole was cruelly accident-prone. When he fell off a stage in Chico, California, it seemed a symbol of his performance. Some felt they would rather vote for Elizabeth Dole than for her husband. Bill Clinton, meanwhile, campaigned with the panache he has always shown.

Clinton achieved a solid victory—almost half the national vote. However, the reelected president faced plenty of problems. He once again confronted a Republican-dominated Congress, and scandals old and new still hung in the air. But 1996 was Bill Clinton's year.

The incumbent: President Clinton signs a bill raising the minimum wage by 20 percent.

The challenger: Bob Dole in Montana, three weeks before he clinched the GOP nomination.

Running mate: Dole's partner Jack Kemp.

Running mate: Confident Al Gore (center).

Family: The Clintons rafting in Wyoming.

The Republican candidates

Ex-governor Lamar Alexander pulled out of the race in March.

Pat Buchanan came closest to threatening Dole's candidacy.

Steve Forbes campaigned on a 17 percent flat tax platform.

The winner: Bill Clinton receives a warm welcome in St. Louis, Missouri. He remained popular throughout his campaign.

Wife: The first lady performs for US troops stationed in Tuzla.

Wife: Elizabeth Dole with husband Bob on his 73rd birthday.

Atlanta goes for the gold

THE CENTENNIAL Olympic Games came to Atlanta in 1996, thanks to the tireless efforts of local real-estate lawyer Billy Payne. It seemed to many an unlikely location for such a massive event, but there is no doubt in the minds of Georgians that the city succeeded.

The bomb in Centennial Park, which killed two and injured 111, will remain a blot on the memory of the Games. And some foreigners griped about excessive commercialization, inadequate bus services, and glitches in the IBM results system. But with a US medal tally topping 100, the US loved the Games.

Outstanding moments

The memories that will linger longest are two outstanding examples of courage, moral and physical. First it was Muhammad Ali at the opening ceremony, proving he is still "the Greatest" by lighting the Olympic flame despite the terrible ravages of Parkinson's disease. Then it was tiny Kerri Strug, the young gymnast who leapt the pain barrier to perform with a damaged ankle and won the admiration of America.

The basketball Dream Team failed to satisfy its admirers and baseball was not a US gold. But there was no lack of superlative athletic performances to cheer. Top of the list has to be Michael Johnson, winner of both the 400 meters and 200 meters, breaking a world record that had stood for 17 years. Carl Lewis became the first person to win gold medals in four consecutive Olympic Games.

Foreign triumphs

Americans were reluctant to take too much interest in foreign triumphs, but Canada's Donovan Bailey was unbeatable in the 100 meters, and South African Josia Thugwane's victory in the men's marathon capped the Games.

Many observers felt the Olympics had become too big, and there were complaints about some new events— beach volleyball, for example, did not strike everyone as a self-evidently valid Olympic sport. But the world had indeed come to Atlanta, and fulfilled Billy Payne's dream.

Concentration: Lisa Leslie helps the US women's basketball team beat Japan.

Triumph: Michael Johnson sets a new world record of 19.32 seconds in the 200 meters.

Drama: Canada's Donovan Bailey is first across the 100-meters finish line, setting a new world record of 9.84 seconds.

Novelty: The US women's beach volleyball team compete at the new Olympic sport.

Tears: US freestyle wrestler Kurt Angle breaks down after winning gold in the 100 kg/220 lb.

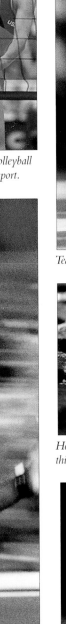

Heroine: Ireland's Michelle Smith wins a third gold in the 200-meters medley.

Courage: Kerri Strug contributes to the US women's gymnastics team victory.

Muscle: Russia's Andrei Chemerkin clinches gold with a 260-kg/572-lb world-record lift.

The people's Olympics

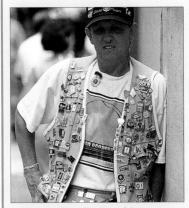

A pin trader displays his acquisitions at the Games.

A statuesque performance artist draws glances from the crowd.

The specially built stadium will serve Atlanta for years to come.

A visitor marks the Centennial Games in idiosyncratic style.

A year of sports triumphs

THE YEAR IN SPORTS was dominated, inevitably, by the Olympics, but domestic sports also had their memorable record-breaking feats and triumphs.

Basketball was dominated by the Chicago Bulls, who created a new record of 72 wins in the regular season and predictably won the NBA Finals. The baseball season was the first to hit the button for years. Batters dominated pitchers, with the Orioles breaking the record for home runs in a season with 257 runs. The Yankees' comeback to snatch the World Series will long be remembered.

Figure skating had strong appeal this year, and US skaters dominated the world championship in Canada. Golf produced a surprise win for Steve Jones in the Open. And Evander Holyfield created one of boxing's greatest upsets by defeating Mike Tyson.

Wonder horse Cigar: Wins 16 straight victories before losing in the Pacific Classic in August.

Todd Eldredge, world figure skating champion.

The Pittsburgh Steelers give the Dallas Cowboys a hard fight for the Super Bowl trophy in January. It was the Cowboys' third Super Bowl victory in four years.

Michelle Kwan: Wins the women's world figure skating title in Edmonton, Canada.

Michael Jordan: MVP in the NBA finals, the regular season, and the All-Star game.

The glittering prizes

Steve Jones with the US Open trophy he won at Oakland Hills.

Cowboys' coach Barry Switzer holds the Super Bowl trophy.

Mike Tyson displays the World Boxing Championship belt he won in March.

The Yankees' Bernie Williams.

Cleveland Indians' Albert Belle: his reputation for big hitting and bad behavior increased.

The Chicago Bulls celebrate their NBA trophy victory.

11

Celebrities in the news

ONE OF THE MOST prominent personalities of the year was an actor who, tragically, no longer acts. Christopher Reeve was a tireless campaigner behind the scenes and a brave presence at many of the year's major public events.

Madonna was, as ever, in the headlines. The year started with her giving evidence against a stalker—by its close she was a new mother. Meanwhile, a new generation of female stars has risen up, including Sandra Bullock, star of one of the year's biggest movie hits, *A Time to Kill*, and the coolly sophisticated Gwyneth Paltrow.

As usual, celebrity marriages proved vulnerable. The world-famous tenor Luciano Pavarotti left his wife of 35 years, and Lisa Marie Presley left her pop-star husband Michael Jackson. In November the controversial Jackson surprisingly announced that he was to become a father.

Madonna, with a new look for Evita *and a new life as the mother of daughter Lourdes.*

John F. Kennedy Jr. and Carolyn Bessette: Confounded journalists by marrying in secret.

Determined to overcome his paralysis, Christopher Reeve goes yachting with his wife Dana and his three children.

Princess Diana visits Washington to pursue her tireless work for medical charities.

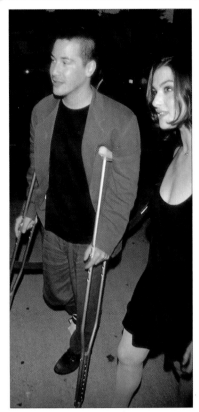

Keanu Reeves on crutches after receiving corrective surgery on an ankle injury.

Tom Cruise stars in the movie version of the TV hit Mission: Impossible.

Sandra Bullock: Confirmed her place as one of the new generation of Hollywood stars.

Gwyneth Paltrow and Brad Pitt: Now a noted Hollywood item. Paltrow won plaudits for her performance in the movie Emma, *based on the Jane Austen novel.*

Opera singer Luciano Pavarotti and his new partner, Nicoletta Mantovani, age 26.

Canadian singer Alanis Morisette won four Grammy awards.

Over a million people paid to see singer Garth Brooks on tour.

Hootie & the Blowfish rode high in the album charts.

Sheryl Crow offended Wal-Mart with lyrics attacking gun sales.

No longer with us

Gene Kelly, February 2

Claudette Colbert, July 30

François Mitterand, January 8

Edmund Muskie, March 26

Dorothy Lamour, September 22

Ella Fitzgerald, June 15

George Burns, March 9

Timothy Leary, May 31

They died this year

January 8, François Mitterand
French socialist politician, president of France from 1981 to 1995.

January 17, Barbara Jordan
Texas Congresswoman who became nationally prominent in the 1970s.

January 29, Joseph Brodsky
Exiled Russian poet, winner of the 1987 Nobel Prize for Literature.

February 2, Gene Kelly
Dancer and actor, star of *Singin' in the Rain* and *An American in Paris*.

February 16, Pat Brown
Democratic governor of California from 1959 to 1967.

March 9, George Burns
Popular comedian, best remembered for his double act with wife Gracie Allen.

March 26, Edmund Muskie
Democratic senator who was a vice-presidential candidate in 1968.

April 3, Ronald Brown
US Commerce Secretary and former chairman of the Democratic party.

April 9, Richard Condon
Thriller writer, author of *Prizzi's Honor* and *The Manchurian Candidate*.

April 28, William J. Colby
Former intelligence agent who headed the CIA in the mid-1970s.

May 31, Timothy Leary
Harvard psychologist who championed the use of psychedelic drugs.

June 15, Ella Fitzgerald
Legendery jazz singer who perfected "scat" singing in the 1940s.

July 12, John Chancellor
Veteran newsman, anchor of *NBC Nightly News* from 1970 to 1982.

July 30, Claudette Colbert
Parisian-born screen star best known for her roles in screwball comedies.

September 16, McGeorge Bundy
Former national security adviser to presidents Kennedy and Johnson.

September 17, Spiro Agnew
Vice President under Richard Nixon who resigned in disgrace in 1973.

September 22, Dorothy Lamour
Sultry actress, co-star of Bob Hope and Bing Crosby's "Road" movies.

October 5, Seymour Cray
Computer pioneer who developed the first transistor-based computer.

October 12, René Lacoste
Tennis star whose nickname—alligator—became the motif for his sports shirts.

November 14, Cardinal Bernardin
Archbishop of Chicago, one of the most respected figures in the Catholic Church.

1996

A week-by-week review of the key events of the year

How the review works

The week-by-week review presents the events of 1996 as they were reported in the media at the time they happened. It allows you to follow events as they unfolded through the year. Many news stories are linked to follow-up items identified by date. The links look like this: (→ February 17). They can lead either to an entry in the weekly summary panels on the left of each double page or to one of the fuller news reports.

S	M	T	W	T	F	S
	1	2	3	4	5	6
7	8	9	10	11	12	13
14	15	16	17	18	19	20
21	22	23	24	25	26	27
28	29	30	31			

Pasadena, CA, 1
Northwestern is defeated 41-32 by Southern California in college football's Rose Bowl.

Texas and Oklahoma, 1
Laws take effect allowing permit holders to carry concealed weapons.

Miami, FL, 1
Dade County curfew requires children under 17 to be indoors by 11 p.m. Sunday through Thursday.

Savannah, GA, 2
Savannah's first black mayor, Floyd Adams Jr., is inaugurated.

New York, 2
AT&T announces it will split into three separate companies and cut 40,000 jobs, at a cost of $6 billion.

Lumberton, NC, 3
The trial begins of Daniel Andre Green, accused of killing the father of basketball star Michael Jordan. (→ February 29)

Washington, DC, 4
The Congressional panel investigating the 1993 firing of White House travel office staff reveals a memo linking the dismissals to Hillary Clinton. (→ January 5)

Norwich, England, 4
A report from the University of East Anglia says that last year was the hottest ever recorded, apparent confirmation of global warming.

Tokyo, 5
Japanese prime minister Tomiichi Murayama announces he is to resign. (→ January 11)

Washington, DC, 5
Hillary Clinton's billing records from the Rose Law Firm, crucial evidence in the Whitewater affair, are released by the White House—after being missing for two years. (→ January 12)

San Francisco, 6
The Green Bay Packers defeat the defending Super Bowl champions the San Francisco 49ers, 27-17, to proceed to the NFC championship.

Deaths
January 1. Admiral Arleigh A. Burke, World War II hero and subsequent chief of naval operations, at age 94, in Bethesda, Maryland.

BOSNIA, TUESDAY 2

US troops pour into Bosnia

US troops make their way across the pontoon bridge from Croatia into Bosnia.

US ground forces are taking up their positions in northeastern Bosnia today as the NATO peacekeeping mission begins in earnest.

On Sunday US Army engineers completed a 650-yd pontoon bridge over the Sava River, which divides Bosnia from Croatia. Hampered by rain, snow, and mud, the engineers had taken longer to complete the structure than expected. As soon as it was finished units of the First Cavalry Brigade, First Armored Division began riding across from Zupanja on the Croatian side to Orasje in Bosnia.

Eventually 20,000 US troops will occupy the Posavina corridor that separates Serb and Muslim Bosnian territory. They will help enforce the peace accord negotiated in Dayton, Ohio, last November. (→ January 13)

WASHINGTON, DC, FRIDAY 5

Republican retreat ends the longest government shutdown

Democrats are claiming victory today in the budget crisis that has caused a partial shutdown of the US government. Bowing to public opinion, the Republican-dominated House of Representatives voted to release funds that would allow federal workers to be paid and most services to resume, at least for the time being.

For 21 days the Republicans in Congress had refused to authorize funding for the everyday business of government in an attempt to force Clinton to accept their proposals for a balanced federal budget by 2002.

About 280,000 federal workers had been sent on unpaid vacation and another 480,000 were working without pay. Services from food programs for the elderly to access to national parks were curtailed as funds ran out.

The government will be back at work on Monday, but negotiations on the budget issue will continue.

Al Gore and Bill Clinton discuss the budget with House leader Newt Gingrich.

GENEVA, THURSDAY 4

Physicists create antimatter

A physicist at the CERN laboratory, where the antimatter atoms were created.

A team of European physicists has created the first complete atoms of antimatter ever to exist. The 11 atoms of antihydrogen were made at the European Laboratory for Particle Physics, known as CERN, last September. The antiatoms only existed for billionths of a second before being wiped out by collisions with ordinary atoms.

Antimatter is the opposite of matter in all its characteristics—it has a negative electric charge where matter has a positive one, for example.

Any practical use for antimatter seems remote at the moment, although the history of nuclear physics in our century suggests that it should not be ruled out.

GAZA, FRIDAY 5

Hamas bomber killed by booby trap

Hamas explosives expert Yahya Ayyash, formerly Israel's enemy number one.

Bomb expert Yahya Ayyash, known as "the Engineer," was the mastermind behind many terrorist bombings that Israel has suffered in the last two years. Today he is dead, himself a victim of a murderous explosion.

Ayyash was killed by a small but deadly explosive charge packed into a mobile phone. It is believed that the booby-trap phone was prepared by the Israeli secret service, who had Ayyash at the top of their wanted list.

A member of the extremist Islamic group Hamas, Ayyash was 32 years old. His death took place in the Gaza Strip, now under the control of Yassir Arafat's PLO.

A Hamas militant warned: "The Hamas brigades will reach the hand that was behind this crime and will deal with it as it should be dealt with."

At the funeral of Yahya Ayyash, thousands of Hamas supporters mob his coffin.

Los Angeles, Wednesday 3. Pop star Madonna testified in court today against stalker Robert Dewey Hoskins. Hoskins allegedly twice entered the grounds of Madonna's home, said he intended to marry her, and threatened to cut her throat "from ear to ear." (→ January 8)

RIYADH, MONDAY 1

Ailing Saudi ruler hands control to his brother

King Fahd of Saudi Arabia has handed over the management of all government affairs to his half-brother, Prince Abdullah. King Fahd is 74 years old and suffered a severe stroke last November.

The stability of Saudi Arabia, the world's largest oil exporter, is of vital importance to Western powers. The Saudis have repeatedly upheld Western interests in the Middle East, notably during the Desert Storm operation against Iraq in 1991. Prince Abdullah is thought to favor a less pro-US policy than the king. (→ February 21)

Crown Prince Abdullah (left) and his half-brother King Fahd (waving).

Sonoita, Mexico, Monday 1. A head-on collision between two buses on New Year's day killed 26 people and injured 24. The crash occurred on a road in northern Mexico, near the Arizona border.

TEMPE, AZ, TUESDAY 2

Nebraska stay champions with rout of Florida

The Nebraska Cornhuskers won their second successive national college football championship in the Tostitos Fiesta Bowl tonight. Florida was expected to at least challenge Nebraska, but a final score of 62-24 proved otherwise.

Despite Nebraska's winning season, coach Tom Osborne described 1995 as "a mixed year." Running-back Lawrence Phillips was suspended for six games after assaulting an ex-girlfriend, and two other players face serious firearms charges.

S	M	T	W	T	F	S
	1	2	3	4	5	6
7	8	9	10	11	12	13
14	15	16	17	18	19	20
21	22	23	24	25	26	27
28	29	30	31			

Los Angeles, 8
Robert Dewey Hoskins is found guilty of stalking pop star Madonna and assaulting her bodyguard.

Guatemala, 8
Alvaro Arzu, leader of the National Advancement party, wins the Guatemalan presidential elections.

Kinshasa, Zaire, 8
A Russian cargo plane crashes into a crowded street market, killing almost 300 people.

St. Louis, MO, 9
A federal appeals court rules that the sexual harassment suit filed against President Clinton by former Arkansas state employee Paula Jones can proceed to trial. (→ June 24)

San Francisco, 9
Willy Brown, first black mayor of San Francisco, says in his inaugural address that "we must unite."

Bosnia, 9
A rocket-propelled grenade hits a streetcar in the city of Sarajevo, killing one civilian.

Haiti, 10
The US confirms that its troops will leave Haiti on February 29, despite a call by the Haitian president-elect René Preval for an extension of the US presence.

Tokyo, 11
Ryutaru Hashimoto is sworn in as the new prime minister of Japan.

Rome, 11
Lamberto Dini resigns as Italian prime minister. (→ February 1)

Miami, 11
Jimmy Johnson has agreed to coach the Miami Dolphins, following the retirement last week of Don Shula. According to the *Miami Herald*, Johnson will be the highest-paid coach in the history of the NFL. (→ September 1)

Deaths
January 7. Karoly Grosz, former reformist communist leader of Hungary, at age 65.

January 8. François Mitterrand, former president of France, at age 79.

NEW YORK, MONDAY 8

Blizzard sweeps the East Coast

Cross-country skiing is the best way of getting down snow-covered Park Avenue.

Snow blankets New York City.

This was the day set for government employees to return to work after the politicians at last ended the federal shutdown. However, Mother Nature had other ideas.

Starting Saturday night, the East Coast was swept by a blizzard described by the National Weather Service as "of historic proportions." By this morning, normal life had come to a halt from Virginia to Massachusetts. Airports are closed, and only snowplows and four-wheel drives are holding the roads. City streets have been abandoned to pedestrians and the occasional urban skier.

The snowfall looks set to be the heaviest in Washington since 1922 and the third heaviest ever recorded in New York. In the city of Philadelphia, which has experienced a record fall of 30.7 in, the authorities have ordered drivers to stay off the streets.

By this evening the blizzard was drifting away northward, but experts warn that more snow is on the way.

PERVOMAYSKAYA, DAGESTAN, THURSDAY 11

Chechen "Lone Wolf" defies the Russian Bear

Chechen rebels are trapped by Russian forces at the border village of Pervomayskaya.

A band of Chechen separatists and their hostages have been encircled by Russian forces in a small village in Dagestan, close to the Chechen border. The band's leader Salman Raduyev, known as the "Lone Wolf," is demanding free passage to the safety of the Chechen mountains.

On Tuesday the rebels seized a hospital in the Dagestani town of Kizlyar, taking 200 hostages. They set out for Chechnya in buses but were attacked by Russian forces short of the border.

Trapped inside the small village of Pervomayskaya, Raduyev has vowed that he and his men will die rather than surrender. (→ January 18)

JARNAC, FRANCE, THURSDAY 11

Mitterrand is mourned by wife and mistress

Mitterrand's final journey is through the streets of his birthplace, Jarnac. He is laid to rest in the family plot in the town's cemetery.

France's former president, François Mitterrand, who died on Monday, returned to his birthplace today. One of Europe's foremost postwar leaders, he was laid to rest in a somber family vault in the small town of Jarnac in southwest France. The ceremony was attended by 500 of his friends and associates. His wife Danielle stood alongside his mistress Anne Pingeot and their daughter Mazarine Pingeot.

In Paris, Mitterrand's passing was commemorated with greater pomp. More than 2,000 people, including heads of state and political leaders from around the world, attended a solemn requiem mass in Notre-Dame cathedral. Al Gore represented the US.

Mitterrand, who was 79 years old, died of prostate cancer. He had been president from 1981 to 1995.

WASHINGTON, DC, FRIDAY 12

Hillary Clinton faces accusations of dishonesty

Hillary Clinton intended to devote this week to publicizing her new book, *It Takes a Village*. Instead, she has to face harsh attacks on her veracity. Opponents are saying that she is, in the blunt words of columnist William Safire, a "congenital liar."

New doubts arose about her role in the Whitewater and Travelgate affairs after documents emerged last week that seem to confirm an involvement the first lady has continually denied. President Clinton continues to give his wife his full backing.

Interviewed by Barbara Walters on ABC's *20/20* this evening, Hillary Clinton said: "Occasionally I get a little distressed, a little sad, a little angry, irritated." She forcefully rejected all the allegations against her. (→ January 26)

Tuzla, Bosnia, Saturday 13. President Clinton, wearing a NATO beret, drops in on the US troops policing the Bosnian cease-fire. Bad weather delayed the president's flight into Tuzla and his stopover there was cut down to three hours. (→ March 25)

CANADA, WEDNESDAY 10

Millionaires vie for balloon record

Branson and his children in his balloon.

British millionaire Richard Branson and US millionaire Steve Fossett are each hoping to become the first person to make a nonstop round-the-world balloon flight.

Steve Fossett, who last year made the first balloon crossing of the Pacific, set off from Rapid City, South Dakota, on Monday during one of America's worst ever winters. But his round-the-world attempt ended ingloriously today in a field near Hampton, New Brunswick, 90 miles beyond the Canadian border.

Fossett blamed a failed power generator for forcing him to abandon the flight. He declared himself "disappointed and embarrassed."

MISSISSIPPI, THURSDAY 11

Student-led prayer unconstitutional

A federal appeals court has ruled that a Mississippi law allowing student-led prayer in public schools is in violation of the constitution, breaching the ban on state-endorsed religion.

Religious right-wing groups had hoped to use the students' right to free speech as a defense, allowing voluntary prayer into the public schools. Teacher-led prayer was banned by the Supreme Court in 1962.

Mexico City, Sunday 7. Keiko, the whale who starred in the film *Free Willy*, was flown from an amusement park in Mexico City to an aquarium in Newport, Oregon, today. He may be released into the ocean.

S	M	T	W	T	F	S
	1	2	3	4	5	6
7	8	9	10	11	12	13
14	15	16	17	18	19	20
21	22	23	24	25	26	27
28	29	30	31			

Irving, TX, 14
The Dallas Cowboys beat the Green Bay Packers to take the NFC championship. In the AFC title game, the Pittsburgh Steelers beat the Indianapolis Colts. (→ January 28)

Lisbon, 14
Socialist Jorge Sampaio wins national election to succeed Mario Soares as president of Portugal.

Mexico City, 15
Top Mexican drug trafficker Juan Garcia Abrego is arrested by Mexican police. He is one of the FBI's ten most-wanted fugitives.

Athens, 15
Andreas Papandreou resigns as Greek prime minister. He is succeeded by Costas Simitis.

Moscow, 16
Anatoli Chubais, leading economic reformer in the Russian government, resigns as deputy prime minister after differences with President Boris Yeltsin. (→ January 29)

Milan, 17
Silvio Berlusconi, Italian media tycoon and former prime minister, goes on trial for corruption.

Oslo, 17
Four men are jailed for stealing Edvard Munch's masterpiece, *The Scream*, in February 1994.

New York, 18
Blind Sheikh Omar Abdel Rahman is sentenced to life imprisonment for plotting terrorist acts in the US. Nine of his associates also receive long prison terms.

Istanbul, 19
The four Chechen gunmen who had hijacked a ferry on the Black Sea surrender to the Turkish authorities.

Deaths
January 15. Moshoeshoe II, king of the southern African state of Lesotho.

January 18. Rudolph Wanderone Jr., known as Minnesota Fats, legendary pool hustler, in Nashville, Tennessee, at age 83.

IOWA, MONDAY 15

Steve Forbes makes his mark

As the competition to select the Republican candidate for the next presidential election gathers momentum, Steve Forbes, a millionaire and a political outsider, is grabbing the limelight. Most polls currently place him second to Bob Dole, and his importance can be measured by the heavy fire he is drawing. At a candidates' forum in Iowa this weekend all the other contenders were united in condemning Forbes as too inexperienced, too remote, and too risky to ever be president.

Steve Forbes's slice of the Forbes family fortune has been estimated by *Fortune* magazine at $439 million. He is using this wealth to buy air time, and he appears to be getting his message across to the public.

Forbes's keynote idea is the 17 percent flat tax. A Republican study commission endorsed the principle of a flat tax today and several Republican candidates have similar plans. But it is Forbes who has succeeded in making the flat-tax platform his own. Despite being dismissed by other candidates as "nutty," the simplicity of Forbes's proposals has struck a nerve with voters who feel oppressed by the complexity of the revenue system. (→ February 7)

Forbes chases Republican nomination.

SAN ANTONIO, TX, TUESDAY 16

Hubble telescope multiplies number of galaxies by five

The American Astronomical Society has today made public the most detailed photographs ever made of a slice of the universe.

Taken over a ten-day period by the Hubble Space Telescope, the photographs radically alter the accepted view of the number of galaxies in the universe. Instead of 10 billion, there appear to be at least 50 billion galaxies.

Varieties of galaxy shown in the photographs are also new to science. A modest galaxy like our own Milky Way contains 50 to 100 billion stars.

Space Shuttle Endeavour, Monday 15. Astronaut Daniel Barry works in the space shuttle's cargo bay during the first of two extravehicular activities scheduled during the space mission.

Austin, TX, Wednesday 17. Barbara Jordan has died at 59. A Congresswoman from Texas, Jordan came to national prominence during the Watergate hearings in 1974.

LONDON, WEDNESDAY 17

Queen of England says she will not pay Duchess of York's debts

Apparently exasperated by her daughter-in-law's lavish spending, Queen Elizabeth II is refusing to provide extra cash to bail her out of debts that some believe are as high as $5 million.

"The Queen has already made generous provisions to the Duchess of York," a spokeswoman said. "It is up to the duchess and her financial advisers to find a solution and it's not a matter for the Queen." Since her separation from Prince Andrew, the duchess is reckoned to have an income of $500,000 a year, but expenses in excess of $800,000.

The Duchess of York faces high debts.

DAGESTAN, THURSDAY 18

Chechen rebels slaughtered

George Burns, comedy legend, is 100 years old

More than 150 Chechen rebels were reported to have been killed by Russian forces as the siege of the village of Pervomayskaya, Dagestan, came to an end. But more than 100 Chechens, including the rebel leader "Lone Wolf" Salman Raduyev, appear to have escaped. It is also feared that many of the bodies found in the village may be those of hostages. The Chechens were holding about 100 hostages when they were trapped by the Russians last week.

President Boris Yeltsin has declared the crisis over and claimed a victory over the rebels. But the Russian media have been heavily critical of the inefficiency of military operations. Efforts by Russian elite troops to take the village were a farcical failure. Soldiers complained of poor leadership and lack of support. Twenty-six Russian soldiers are reported killed in the fighting and another 93 wounded. On

Comic George Burns.

One of the US's best loved comedians, George Burns, is 100 years old today. Burns had planned to put on a show in Las Vegas for his centenary birthday. Tickets for the event were already sold when a fall in a bath in July 1994 made him too frail.

Born in New York as Nathan Birnbaum, Burns married Gracie Allen in 1925. The *George Burns and Gracie Allen Show* was a fixture of 1950s' TV. Gracie has been dead for more than 20 years, but George is still wisecracking and smoking the cigars—El Producto Queens—that became his trademark. (→ March 9)

Pervomayskaya after the Russian attack; some of the bodies may be those of hostages.

Chechen gunman with ferry hostages.

Wednesday the Russians resorted to pounding Pervomayskaya with indiscriminate Grad rocket fire, reducing the village to ruins.

In a separate incident on Tuesday, Chechen gunmen hijacked a ferry in the Black Sea and forced it to sail from Trabzon in Turkey toward the Bosphorus. About 200 passengers, most of them Russians, were being held hostage. The gunmen were demanding an end to the siege of the village of Pervomayskaya. They may end the hijacking now that their demands no longer apply.

Russia enjoys the full support of the US administration for its use of military force to counter hostage taking and acts of terrorism by the Chechen rebels. (→ January 19)

A Chechen commando tries to negotiate with Russian forces during the siege.

Los Angeles, Thursday 18. Lisa Marie Presley has filed for divorce from singer Michael Jackson. The couple have been married for 15 months.

S	M	T	W	T	F	S
	1	2	3	4	5	6
7	8	9	10	11	12	13
14	15	16	17	18	19	20
21	22	23	24	25	26	27
28	29	30	31			

Pennsylvania, 21
The state is declared a disaster area after the worst flooding in more than 20 years. Much of New Jersey, Maryland, New York state, Virginia, Ohio, and West Virginia is also swamped by a combination of melting snow and heavy rains.

Bosnia, 21
US assistant secretary of state for human rights John Shattuck visits the site of alleged mass graves in the Srebrenica area of Bosnia.

Netherlands, 23
The Dutch aircraft manufacturer Fokker, facing bankruptcy, files for protection from its creditors.

New York, 23
The World Health Organization recommends that the two remaining stocks of smallpox virus be destroyed before the end of the century. Smallpox was declared eradicated as a disease in 1980.

Seoul, South Korea, 23
Two former presidents of South Korea, Chun Doo-hwan and Roh Tae-woo, are indicted for treason in connection with the violent suppression of pro-democracy demonstrations in 1980. (→ March 11)

Belfast, 24
The Mitchell Commission, headed by US senator George Mitchell, advises that negotiations on the future of Northern Ireland should proceed without the IRA and other paramilitaries first disarming. (→ February 28)

Warsaw, 24
Polish prime minister Jozef Oleksy resigns after allegations that he worked as a Russian spy. (→ February 1)

New York, 24
Wells Fargo & Co. acquires First Interstate Bancorp to create the eighth-largest bank in the US.

New York, 24
Computer company Apple denies a report that it is to be bought by Sun Microsystems. (→ February 2)

Strasbourg, 25
The Council of Europe, Europe's leading human rights organization, admits Russia as a member.

Clinton wins applause

President Clinton's State of the Union address gets a warm reception from Congress.

Delivering his State of the Union address to Congress this evening, President Clinton staked his claim to the center ground in American politics. Borrowing many Republican themes, he promised measures to promote family life and crack down on crime, and declared that "the era of big government is over." He also stressed that Congress should keep working for a balanced budget deal. Observers agree that the president radiated confidence, buoyed up by his high standing in the opinion polls.

Congress gave a standing ovation to Hillary Clinton, described by the president as "a wonderful wife, a magnificent mother, and a great first lady." She faces a grand jury hearing later in the week. (→ January 26)

Hillary Clinton sails through grand jury

Hillary Clinton emerged from four hours of questioning by a grand jury today looking calm and unruffled. She told the press: "I was very pleased to tell the grand jury what I have been telling all of you. I don't know how the missing papers turned up but, I'm pleased they did because they confirm what I have been saying."

Independent Whitewater prosecutor Kenneth Starr had subpoenaed the first lady to testify about elusive billing records that disappeared for two years and then turned up in the White House. The records give details of Hillary Clinton's legal work for Madison Guaranty, the savings and loan company at the heart of the Whitewater scandal.

Hillary Clinton answers press questions after her grand jury hearing.

Los Angeles, Sunday 21. Nicolas Cage (above left), star of *Leaving Las Vegas*, tonight won the Golden Globe award for best actor in a drama. Emma Thompson's movie *Sense and Sensibility* (above right) took awards for best drama and best screenplay. Other winners included Jimmy Smits of *NYPD Blue* for best TV actor and Nicole Kidman for best movie comedy actress.

JERUSALEM, SUNDAY 21

Arafat triumphs in first Palestinian elections

Yasir Arafat participating in Gaza airport's inauguration ceremony the day before Palestinians turn out to vote.

Yasir Arafat and his Fatah movement have triumphed in elections that could be a major step toward Palestinian statehood. Palestinians in the West Bank, Gaza, and in East Jerusalem voted yesterday to elect a president and a legislative council to run the Palestinian autonomous areas, granted self-rule by Israel as part of the Middle East peace process.

In his quest for the presidency, Arafat won around 88 percent of the votes cast. Fatah candidates took 50 seats in the 88-seat Palestinian council. An exultant Arafat declared: "This is a new era. This is the foundation of our Palestinian state."

The militant Islamic movement Hamas, which rejects the peace process, called on voters to boycott the elections, but this was widely ignored. International observers were worried by cases of intimidation during the campaign. But they agreed that the vote could be "regarded as an accurate expression of the will of the voters on polling day." (→ February 12)

UTAH, FRIDAY 26

Killer executed by firing squad

The chair at Utah's state prison in which Taylor was executed by firing squad.

Killer John Albert Taylor was executed by firing squad at 12:03 a.m. today in Utah state prison. Taylor had been convicted of the 1989 rape and murder of 11-year-old Charla King.

The prison authorities were quietly satisfied by the efficiency of an execution that had attracted widespread media attention. "The blood spatter was very minimal," said one official. Five marksmen fired on Taylor, although only four of the weapons were loaded.

MOUNTAIN VIEW, CA, MONDAY 22

Galileo springs Jupiter surprise

The Galileo space probe that plunged into the gaseous atmosphere of Jupiter last December has overturned many scientific ideas about the planet.

It appears that there is only half the helium that was expected in Jupiter's atmosphere. Winds are stronger but skies are clearer. There is very little water and no lightning.

Release of the data from the probe had been delayed by the US government shutdown that put NASA's Research Center at Mountain View, California, on enforced furlough.

Seattle, Thursday 25. Sonam Wangdu, the four-year-old boy thought by Buddhist monks to be the reincarnation of the Dalai Lama, leaves Seattle today for years of study in a Nepal monastery. His American mother, Carolyn Lama, will see him only twice a year.

WASHINGTON, DC, WED. 24

O. J. Simpson gives TV interview

For the first time since his acquittal on double murder charges, O. J. Simpson was interviewed on television tonight. But his conversation with newscaster Ed Gordon on the cable network Black Entertainment Television failed to shed new light on the case.

Simpson refused to answer several key questions, referring viewers to a $29.95 video he is marketing that gives his version of events. The interviewer suggested it would be better if he would "tell America something for free." The video was advertised throughout the program. Simpson claimed that he needed the money because he has a family to support.

Simpson attacked the attitude of the families of murder victims Nicole Brown and Ronald Goldman. "I have a side of me that is very angry at Fred Goldman [Ronald Goldman's father] and the Browns," he said. Simpson faces a civil suit for wrongful death, brought by the victims' families, who do not accept the not-guilty verdict.

January

S	M	T	W	T	F	S
	1	2	3	4	5	6
7	8	9	10	11	12	13
14	15	16	17	18	19	20
21	22	23	24	25	26	27
28	29	30	31			

Johannesburg, 28
Nation of Islam leader Louis Farrakhan meets with South African president Nelson Mandela.

Canberra, 28
Australian prime minister Paul Keating calls parliamentary elections for March 2. (→ March 3)

Melbourne, 28
In the Australian Open tennis championships, Boris Becker defeats Michael Chang to win the men's singles, and Monica Seles wins the women's title, defeating Anke Huber.

Niamey, Niger, 28
An army coup in the francophone West African state of Niger brings the armed forces chief of staff, Colonel Ibrahim Bare Mainassara, to power.

Paris, 29
French president Jacques Chirac announces an end to the French underground nuclear-test program that had provoked worldwide protests.

Johannesburg, 29
Eight people are killed and 23 wounded when gunmen open fire on jobseekers outside a factory.

Los Angeles, 30
Country star Garth Brooks declines to take the American Music Award trophy for artist of the year, saying: "I cannot agree with this."

Chicago, 30
Two juveniles who dropped five-year-old Eric Morse to his death from a 14th-floor window are sentenced to an indefinite term in a youth prison. Age 10 and 11 at the time of the killing, the boys dropped Morse because he refused to steal candy.

Portland, OR, 31
Democratic candidate Ron Wyden wins the race for Oregon's vacant Senate seat by 1 percent from Republican Gordon Smith. Wyden is the first Democrat elected to represent Oregon in the Senate since 1962.

Deaths
January 28. Jerry Siegel, one of the creators of Superman, in Los Angeles, at age 81.

January 29. Joseph Brodsky, Russian-born writer, in New York, at age 55.

PENNSYLVANIA, SUNDAY 28

Du Pont arrested for murder of Olympic wrestler

John Eleuthere du Pont, a member of one of the richest families in the US, was arrested today, suspected of killing Olympic gold-medal wrestler Dave Schultz.

Schultz was shot dead Friday on du Pont's estate at Newton Square, Pennsylvania. The arrest came after a 48-hour standoff between du Pont and the police. Du Pont, an expert marksman, had barricaded himself inside his mansion. He was grabbed when he came outside to inspect his boiler, which the police had switched off.

John du Pont built the Delaware Museum of Natural History and managed the US Olympic pentathlon team in 1976. The millionaire is also a wrestling enthusiast, and he used his fortune to build and fund an Olympic training center for wrestlers on his estate. Schultz was one of a team of athletes living and training there.

But du Pont is also known for his eccentric behavior, which neighbors claimed had worsened in recent months. Allegations are emerging that last year he banned African-American athletes from his estate, claiming that the color black reminded him of death. (→ May 31)

JERUSALEM, SUNDAY 28

Ethiopian Jews riot over Israeli AIDS policy

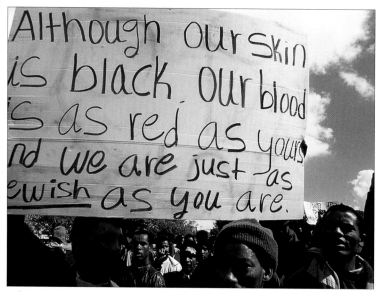

Ethiopian Jews protest at what they perceive as racism in Israel's AIDS policy.

In Jerusalem today riot police fought with crowds of Ethiopian Jews who were angered by the revelation that Ethiopian blood was being dumped from Israeli blood banks.

Tear gas and water cannons were used in an effort to disperse the crowd, who had surrounded the office of Prime Minister Shimon Peres. Protestors retaliated by throwing rocks, smashing car windows, and injuring dozens of police. The fighting lasted for several hours.

The authorities claim that blood donated by Ethiopians has too high a risk of infection from the HIV virus that causes AIDS. The Ethiopians, 60,000 of whom have arrived in Israel since 1984, believe they are the victims of primitive racism. They claim they are also discriminated against in housing and employment.

Arizona, Sunday 28. The Dallas Cowboys beat the Pittsburgh Steelers 27-17 in Super Bowl XXX, watched by TV viewers in 150 countries. It was the Cowboys' third Super Bowl win in four years.

HAIPHONG, SUNDAY 28

Vietnam jails US war veteran for five years

Everett Sennholz, a US veteran of the Vietnam War, has been sentenced to five years in prison by a Vietnamese court. Sennholz had first returned to Vietnam for a short visit in 1992. He later decided to settle in Haiphong, intending to marry a Vietnamese woman.

Sennholz was arrested in August last year when a rifle and a shotgun were found among goods he was bringing into Vietnam. He was also charged for importing books and tapes presenting an American viewpoint on the Vietnam War.

COLOMBO, SRI LANKA, WEDNESDAY 31
Tamil Tigers devastate capital

Colombo's Central Bank—the bomb blasted an 8-ft crater in front of the building.

The wounded are carried to safety—more than 1,400 were injured in the blast.

The Liberation Tigers of Tamil Eelam carried out a devastating terrorist attack on the Sri Lankan capital, Colombo, today. A truck loaded with 400 lb of explosives was driven through the gates of the Central Bank, in the heart of the city, at 10:45 a.m. The explosion caused widespread destruction, killing at least 55 people immediately. The death toll is expected to rise.

The majority of Sri Lanka's people are Sinhalese, the minority Tamil. For 13 years, the Tamil Tigers have been fighting for a separate Tamil state. Recently the Sri Lankan army has scored significant successes against the Tigers. This was their response.

NASHVILLE, TN, MONDAY 29
US Navy jet fighter crashes, killing five

A US Navy F-14 Tomcat flying out of Nashville International Airport crashed into a local neighborhood this morning, killing an elderly couple—Elmer and Ada Newsom—as well as their friend Ewing Wair. The two crew of the aircraft were also killed. The pilot, Lieutenant Commander John Stacy Bates, was being watched by his parents as he took off on a training exercise.

This was the thirtieth Navy-Tomcat crash since 1991, and the fourth accident involving Bates's squadron, VF 213, in the last 16 months. (→ April 12)

Venice, Tuesday 30. The 204-year-old Fenice opera house, believed by many to be the most beautiful in the world, was gutted by fire last night. Tenor Luciano Pavarotti told reporters after the fire: "The whole world of opera feels like an orphan." (→ June 26)

WASHINGTON, DC, MON. 29
Russian says reforms go on

Russian prime minister Viktor S. Chernomyrdin, in Washington for a regular committee meeting with US vice president Al Gore, is insisting that economic and political reforms in Russia will continue.

Doubts have been cast over the reform program's fate since leading economic reformer, Deputy Prime Minister Anatoli Chubai, resigned earlier this month. Russia needs a $9-billion IMF loan that will be blocked if doubts about reform persist.

Prime Minister Viktor S. Chernomyrdin.

LOS ANGELES, TUESDAY 30
Magic Johnson is back with Lakers

Four and a half years ago Magic Johnson retired from basketball after testing HIV positive. Tonight he was back with the Los Angeles Lakers.

Before the game, Johnson played down expectations. "I just want to get into the game," he said, "smell the popcorn, get out there and hit somebody, and then I'll know I'm back." He did better than that. Now age 36 and slower than at his peak, Johnson still finished the night with 19 points, 10 assists, and 8 rebounds.

Johnson's performance drew rave reviews. Sportswriters are already betting on Magic and the Lakers to face Michael Jordan and the Chicago Bulls in the NBA finals.

But Johnson himself only expressed dissatisfaction. "What am I really happy about? Nothing yet because I really haven't accomplished anything in my mind. I know with time things will get better." (→ May 14)

S	M	T	W	T	F	S
				1	2	3
4	5	6	7	8	9	10
11	12	13	14	15	16	17
18	19	20	21	22	23	24
25	26	27	28	29		

Warsaw, 1
Wlodzimierz Cimoszewicz, a former communist, is appointed to succeed Jozef Oleksy as Polish prime minister.

Dallas, 1
A new Texan law gives the relatives of murder victims the right to view the execution of the murderer.

Rome, 1
Antonio Maccanico is appointed Italian prime minister in an effort to resolve the country's political crisis.

New York, 2
Gilbert F. Amelio replaces Michael Spindler as chief executive of Apple Computers Inc.

Denver, 4
The Chicago Bulls lose 105-99 to the Denver Nuggets, ending a winning sequence of 18 games.

Dedham, MA, 5
The trial begins of John Salvi, accused of killings at two Brookline abortion clinics in December 1994. (→ March 18)

Los Angeles, 5
O. J. Simpson tells the CNN legal show *Burden of Proof* that he did not abuse his wife Nicole.

Tuzla, Bosnia, 5
NATO announces that the first US peacekeeper to die in Bosnia, Sergeant 1st Class Donald Dugan, was not killed by a mine as first thought, but by ammunition exploding in his hands. Dugan died on February 3.

San Jose, CA, 5
Richard Davis goes on trial for the kidnapping and murder of 12-year-old Polly Klaas in 1993. (→ June 19)

Little Rock, 5
President Clinton is subpoenaed to testify for the defense in the trial of Susan McDougal, one of his former business partners in the failed Whitewater land deal. (→ March 4)

Dominican Republic, 7
A Boeing 757 airliner crashes in the Caribbean, killing 189 people, most of them German tourists.

New York, 8
Dave Winfield announces he is retiring from major league baseball after 23 seasons.

LONDON, SATURDAY 10

London blast shatters the cease-fire

The bomb near South Quays station blows out windows of buildings on the Isle of Dogs and shakes the 800-ft tall Canary Wharf tower.

Just after 7 p.m. this evening, the IRA cease-fire that had brought peace to the British Isles for 17 months came to a sudden and violent end. A bomb planted by the IRA exploded near South Quays railroad station on the Isle of Dogs, devastating a swathe of London's Docklands.

The massive blast was heard up to 8 miles away. Although warnings had been given, hundreds of people were still in the area when the bomb went off. Two have died and many more are injured, some seriously.

The IRA declared it had ended the cease-fire "with great reluctance," claiming it had been driven to it by British "bad faith." Sinn Fein president Gerry Adams said he regretted the breakdown of the cease-fire, but he refused to condemn the bombing.

British prime minister John Major vowed to continue the search for peace. He said: "It would be a tragedy if the hopes of the people of Britain and Northern Ireland for a lasting peace were dashed again by the men of violence." (→ February 12)

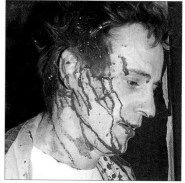

Most victims are injured by flying glass.

Beverly Hills, Friday 2. Gene Kelly, star of the musical *Singin' in the Rain*, dies, at age 83.

WASHINGTON, DC, THURSDAY 1

Congress opens the way to new telecom age

Legislation approved by Congress today is set to transform the structure of the telecommunications business in the US by abolishing many long-standing regulatory barriers. Experts foresee a wave of mergers and layoffs as companies adjust to deregulation.

The new rules will allow long-distance telephone companies into local telephone markets, and local telephone companies to compete for long-distance business. It also allows cable television operators to provide telephone services. The goal, says Representative Edward J. Markey, is a "digital free-for-all."

The bill is liberal in economics but not in morality, however. It makes the transmission of indecent material on the Internet a crime, and requires new television sets to have the "V chip"—a device that allows parents to censor what their children can see on television.

SARAJEVO, BOSNIA, TUESDAY 6

Serb officers suspected of war crimes are arrested

Arrested officers Colonel Aleksa Krsmanovic (left) and General Djordje Djukic.

Two senior Bosnian-Serb officers, General Djukic and Colonel Krsmanovic, have been detained in Sarajevo. The Bosnian government claims they were responsible for the massacre of civilians during the Bosnian War. The officers may stand trial before the War Crimes Tribunal in The Hague.

The Bosnian-Serb authorities have responded by threatening not to implement the Dayton peace accord. (→ February 12)

BEIJING, THURSDAY 8

China's relations with US sail into troubled waters

The Chinese government's aggressive stance on Taiwan is worsening an already strained relationship with the US. Today a Chinese spokesman called on the US to halt major arms sales to Taiwan and reiterated China's intention to invade the island if the Taiwanese government ever declares independence. China is increasing pressure on Taiwan in the buildup to Taiwanese presidential elections.

The US is also in confrontation with China over that country's supply of nuclear-weapons-related equipment to Pakistan. US legislation meant to deter nuclear proliferation requires the president to institute severe trade sanctions against China, but President Clinton is reluctant to anger Beijing and jeopardize US business interests.

Philadelphia, Saturday 10. Chess champion Garry Kasparov lost the first game in his six-game tournament against computer Deep Blue. (→ February 17)

LOUISIANA, WEDNESDAY 7

Buchanan victory upsets Gramm

Pat Buchanan has emerged as the leading conservative contender for the Republican presidential nomination by winning the Louisiana caucuses at the expense of Phil Gramm. Both belong to the antiabortion, isolationist wing of the Republican party. Gramm was relying on support in the South to boost his campaign and had expected to do well in Louisiana.

Neither Bob Dole nor the other leading contender for the Republican candidacy, the multi-millionaire Steve Forbes, contested the Louisiana caucuses. (→ February 13)

EASTERN US, MONDAY 5

Arctic freeze grips the US

The US is frozen from the Midwest eastward to the Atlantic. Milwaukee, Wisconsin, is one of many places registering their coldest day on record. At Ely, Minnesota, the temperature fell to -51°F on Thursday.

Punxsutawney Phil, star of last Friday's Groundhog Day, brought no relief. Phil "saw" his shadow, thereby predicting six more weeks of winter.

Chicago's Lincoln Park: The city woke up to a temperature of -14°F on Monday.

RUSSIA, SATURDAY 3

Yeltsin buys off striking miners

Yeltsin (right), touring Russian mines.

The Russian president Boris Yeltsin has been forced to promise Russian coal miners backwages and subsidies worth around $7 billion to persuade them to end a national strike.

Some 450,000 miners (80 percent of the industry's workforce) had come out in support of their union's demands. The strike lasted two days.

These concessions are yet another blow to Yeltsin's prestige, and raise severe doubts as to whether he can carry through the tough financial cutbacks being demanded by the IMF.

Guatemala, Monday 5. Pope John Paul II was welcomed by thousands of Catholics during his two-day tour of the country.

February

San Antonio, TX, 12
The Eastern Conference beats the Western Conference 129-118 in the NBA All-Star Game. Michael Jordan is booed for winning the most valuable player award, believed by most to be deserved by Shaquille O'Neal.

Gaza, 12
Yasir Arafat takes office as president of the Palestinian Authority.

San Francisco, 13
A study by the San Francisco Center on Juvenile and Criminal Justice claims that, in California, two out of five black males between the ages of 20 and 30 are either imprisoned, on parole, or on probation.

Washington, DC, 14
Senator Phil Gramm withdraws from the race for the Republican presidential nomination. (→ February 21)

Xichang, China, 14
Intelsat announces that a rocket carrying an Intelsat satellite exploded soon after takeoff in China last Thursday.

London, 15
The Scott report on Britain's arms-to-Iraq scandal is published. It accuses ministers of deceiving parliament on arms policy. (→ February 26)

Nevada, 15
Heavyweight boxer Tommy Morrison confirms he has tested HIV positive.

Bogota, 15
President Samper of Colombia is charged with drug-related electoral fraud by the Colombian attorney-general, Alfonso Valdovieso.

Maryland, 17
National Transportation Board officials suggest that human error may have been responsible for the Maryland train disaster.

Rome, 17
Croatian, Bosnian, and Serbian leaders meet with Richard Holbrooke to discuss progress with implementation of the Dayton accord. (→ February 22)

Deaths
February 13. Martin Balsam, film actor, in Rome, at age 76.

February 16. Pat Brown, former governor of California, in Beverly Hills, at age 90.

Maryland train crash kills 11

The wreckage of the Amtrak and MARC trains that collided killing 11 people.

An Amtrak train bound for Chicago and a Maryland Rail Commuter train collided head-on at Silver Spring, Maryland, this evening. Three crew and eight passengers were killed. The Amtrak train had changed tracks to pass a stopped freight train. A fireball incinerated the front car of the commuter train. The eight dead were all young people enrolled in Job Corps, a federal employment training program. (→ February 17)

Dole edges a win over Buchanan in Iowa primary

Senator Bob Dole has won the Iowa primary, but only 3 percent ahead of Pat Buchanan, the conservative commentator. With Steve Forbes and Senator Phil Gramm performing poorly, Buchanan is now clearly the main threat to Dole's candidacy.

Buchanan appeals to the antiabortion, protectionist, anti-immigration wing of the Republicans. He sees himself as fighting "a cultural war for the soul of America." Dole is the chosen representative of the Washington Republican elite. He is trusted, experienced, and well-funded. But his public appearances can be lackluster, and his views are too moderate for many in his own party. Still, few doubt that he will be the Republican presidential candidate. (→ February 14)

Joan Collins wins $3 million from publisher

Joan Collins celebrates her partial victory.

Actress and popular novelist Joan Collins is an estimated $3 million richer today after winning a legal battle with publisher Random House. The publisher had claimed that two manuscripts submitted by Ms. Collins were so badly written they were unpublishable and could not be called "complete." The contract for the two books was worth $4 million.

The jury found that the first work, *The Ruling Passion*, was complete, although the second, *Hell Hath No Fury*, was not. Judge Ira Gammerman, who presided, said the case had been "a joy." Ms. Collins went off to celebrate with champagne.

Dayton accord on brink of failure

US Assistant Secretary of State Richard C. Holbrooke, who last year brokered the Dayton accord that stopped the Bosnian War, was back in the former Yugoslavia this weekend, striving to keep the peace alive.

Bosnian Serbs were threatening to return to confrontation after the arrest of two of their officers, Colonel Aleksa Krsmanovic and General Djordje Djukic. The two men were flown to The Hague today, where they will face the International War Crimes Tribunal.

Holbrooke found a formula to paper over the crisis, laying down rules covering future arrests. Only those on a list of 52 wanted men may be apprehended. The list includes Bosnian Serb political and military leaders Radovan Karadzic and General Ratko Mladic. (→ February 17)

Minneapolis, Thursday 15. The singer formerly known as Prince has married Myte Garcia, a Puerto Rican dancer. Myte referred to the star during the ceremony by pointing to his symbol.

BELFAST, MONDAY 12

Thousands join Irish peace rally

Many of the 3,000-strong crowd wave paper cutouts of the dove, symbol of peace.

Thousands gathered outside Belfast City Hall today to express the desire of the people of Northern Ireland for peace. They were responding to the IRA bombing last week that ended an 18-month cease-fire.

The British prime minister, John Major, gave his own response to the renewed terrorist campaign in a somber five-minute TV broadcast. He said that Sinn Fein, the political wing of the IRA, would be excluded from negotiations on the future of Northern Ireland until the cease-fire was reinstated. "The IRA will never bomb their way to the negotiating table," he said. But he insisted that the search for peace would continue.

Major is anxious to hold elections as a prelude to negotiations, although the Irish leader, John Bruton, said earlier that this would only serve to "pour petrol on the flames." (→ February 18)

MOSCOW, THURSDAY 15

Zhirinovsky flirts with extremists

Ultranationalist Vladimir Zhirinovsky launched his campaign for the Russian presidency today with a lavishly staged silver wedding ceremony at Moscow's Church of St. Michael the Archangel. The star guest was Jean-Marie Le Pen, French National Front leader. Zhirinovsky hopes to boost his prestige by an alliance with European right-wing extremists.

Vladimir Zhirinovsky with wife, Galina.

RIO DE JANEIRO, SUNDAY 11

Michael Jackson video made in Rio slums arouses controversy

Michael Jackson delights residents of Santa Marta during the filming of his new video.

Pop superstar Michael Jackson began filming his latest music video in the slums of Rio de Janeiro today. Directed by Spike Lee, the video "They Don't Care About Us" is set in Santa Marta, one of the *favelas*, crowded shantytowns that tumble chaotically down Rio's steep hillsides.

The poverty of Santa Marta is not the image of Rio that the Brazilian authorities want the world to see. Soccer hero Pele, now minister of sport, said the video could harm the city's bid for the 2004 Olympics. But legal action to stop the filming failed.

The people of Santa Marta are pleased. A local residents' spokesman said, "Thanks to Michael Jackson, our slum is now on the map. His visit here makes a world of difference."

PHILADELPHIA, SATURDAY 17

Kasparov wins "for the human race"

Chess champion Garry Kasparov triumphed over Deep Blue, the top chess computer, at the Pennsylvania Convention Center today. He won the sixth and final game of the eight-day challenge match to finish overall winner by four points to two.

Deep Blue, which can analyze 100 million chess positions a second, had shocked the chess world by defeating Kasparov in the match's first game.

Kasparov called the defeat "the most humiliating experience." The human player then showed superior adaptability, changing his play to exploit the computer's weaknesses.

After the match, Kasparov said: "I did a good job for chess first, and probably for mankind." He had earlier declared that he was playing to defend "human dignity" against the machine.

TEHERAN, TUESDAY 13

Farrakhan addresses Iranian parliament

Black Muslim leader Louis Farrakhan denounced the US in a speech to the Iranian parliament today. Speaking for the Nation of Islam movement, Farrakhan said: "We live in the center of corruption and struggle in the heart of the great Satan." He appealed for Iran's spiritual aid.

Farrakhan is in Iran for the seventeenth anniversary of the Islamic Revolution. His visit comes at a time when the US is trying to coordinate diplomatic action against Iran, which it blames for promoting terrorism.

Los Angeles, Tuesday 13. The career of actor Richard Dreyfuss is enjoying a revival with his much-praised role in *Mr. Holland's Opus*.

February

Gabon, 18
The World Health Organization sends experts to a village in Gabon where ten people have died of the Ebola virus after eating a chimpanzee.

Oklahoma City, 20
A federal judge instructs that the trial of Oklahoma bombing suspects Timothy McVeigh and Terry Nichols should be moved from Lawton, Oklahoma, to Denver, in the interests of a fair trial. (→ July 14)

Orlando Arena, 20
Orlando Magic win their 28th home game out of 28 this season, establishing an NBA record for consecutive home victories at the start of a season.

Washington, DC, 20
Kweise Mfume is sworn in as the president of the NAACP.

Northern Territory, Australia, 21
Northern Territory passes legislation allowing euthanasia in cases where the terminally ill ask to die. (→ July 1)

Riyadh, 21
King Fahd of Saudi Arabia announces that he is resuming full royal duties.

Los Angeles, 21
Rap singer Snoop Doggy Dog, real name Calvin Broadus, and his bodyguard are cleared of the murder of Philip Woldemariam.

Arles, France, 21
Jeanne Calment, 121 years old today, believed to be the oldest person ever, has released a pop CD to celebrate her birthday.

Washington, DC, 22
Alan Greenspan is reappointed to a third term as the chairman of the Federal Reserve.

Los Angeles, 22
O. J. Simpson agrees to share the right to commercial use of the initials "O. J." with the Florida Department of Citrus.

Paris, 22
President Jacques Chirac announces that France is to end conscription and scrap its land-based nuclear weapons.

Deaths
February 21. Morton Gould, American composer and conductor, at age 82.

IRAQ, FRIDAY 23
Returning Iraqi defectors killed

Two sons-in-law of the Iraqi president Saddam Hussein were killed today, only three days after they returned to Iraq from exile in Jordan. Lieutenant-General Hussein Kamel and his brother Saddam Kamel had defected six months ago, vowing to overthrow Saddam Hussein.

The defectors returned to Iraq with their wives after Saddam promised they would be unharmed. Madeleine Albright, US ambassador to the UN, blamed the Iraqi president for the killings, saying "his brutality knows no bounds."

Lahore, Thursday 22. After visiting the Shaukat Kanum cancer hospital today, the Princess of Wales—guest of Pakistani sports star Imran Khan and his wife Jemima—attended a party marking the end of Ramadan. (→ April 14)

LONDON, SUNDAY 18
Bus blown up by IRA in central London

The wreckage of the double-decker bus that was torn apart last night by an IRA bomb.

A powerful explosion ripped apart a bus in the center of London last night, killing at least one person. The dead man is believed to be the bomber, whose explosive device went off prematurely. The explosion occurred at 10:38 p.m. Fortunately the bus was almost empty and there were few passersby. Coming only nine days after the London Docklands bombing, it confirms that the IRA cease-fire is dead and buried.

POTGIETERSRUS, SOUTH AFRICA, THURSDAY 22
Black children escorted into whites-only school

Armed police open the gate of Potgietersrus primary school to a new pupil.

South Africa today passed a new test in racial integration, which brought the small town of Potgietersrus to the attention of the world's media.

Last month white parents formed a human barricade to stop black children from taking their places in the town's whites-only primary school. But on Wednesday a Supreme Court judge upheld an order opening the school to blacks in line with the country's new nonracist principles.

Today, only a few whites stood to watch as armed police escorted black pupils through the school's gates. Still hostile or doubtful, most white parents kept their children home.

WASHINGTON, DC, THURS. 22

Holbrooke leaves the hot seat

Richard C. Holbrooke, the architect of the Dayton accord that stopped the war in Bosnia last year, left his post as assistant secretary of state today for a lucrative vice-chairmanship in a Manhattan bank. Asked whether he thought the peace deal would hold, Holbrooke was noncommittal: "The jury's still out," he said.

Richard Holbrooke, broker of peace accord.

NEW HAMPSHIRE, WEDNESDAY 21

Buchanan wins sensational victory in New Hampshire

Right-wing Republican candidate Pat Buchanan on the campaign trail.

Senator Bob Dole is sore after losing the New Hampshire primary yesterday. Right-wing commentator Pat Buchanan topped the poll, beating Dole by a percentage point, and throwing the Republican nomination contest wide open.

"This is now a race between the mainstream and the extreme," Dole said today, claiming that Buchanan's campaign displayed "an intolerance which I will not tolerate." Buchanan denies extremism. "We are conservatives of the heart," he asserted. (→ February 27)

NEW YORK, WEDNESDAY 21

Primary Colors author mystery solved—or is it?

No question has excited such wild speculation in US political and journalistic circles this year as: Who wrote *Primary Colors*? The best-selling novel, which presents a lightly fictionalized version of recent US political events, was published with "anonymous" on the jacket. Many details in the book led commentators to guess that the author was a White House intimate.

Now according to *New York* magazine, the question is solved. Donald Foster, a literature professor at Vassar College, has applied computer analysis to the text of the book and the writing of possible suspects. Foster concludes that the mystery author is *Newsweek* columnist Joe Klein.

But Klein vigorously denies that he wrote the book. And now it seems that Foster will only say he thinks Klein was a "primary player" who contributed to the book. Meanwhile, the publishers of *Primary Colors*, Random House, insist they do not know the identity of the author, so the speculation continues. (→ July 17)

NEW YORK, WEDNESDAY 21

Scientists find the cause of tobacco addiction

The science journal *Nature* reports that a team of scientists, led by Dr. Joanna Fowler at Brookhaven National Laboratory in New York state, believe they have identified the mechanism of cigarette addiction.

According to the report, smoking reduces by an average 40 percent the quantity of an enzyme, monoamine oxidase B, found in the brain. This in turn increases the quantity of dopamine, a signaling chemical that helps regulate mood and movement. High levels of dopamine are associated with almost all addictive drugs.

A possible practical application of this discovery is the production of a medication that mimics the effect of smoking on the brain. This could be used by addicts to help them kick the habit painlessly.

Daytona Beach, FL, Sunday 18. Dale Jarrett wins the Daytona 500 for the second time, defeating Dale Earnhardt by 0.12 seconds. Jarrett attributed his win to the power of the engine in his Robert Yates Ford. He passed Earnhardt on the 177th lap and held on to the finish.

February

S	M	T	W	T	F	S
				1	2	3
4	5	6	7	8	9	10
11	12	13	14	15	16	17
18	19	20	21	22	23	24
25	26	27	28	29		

Washington, DC, 25
According to US intelligence sources, Libyan leader Colonel Muammar Gadhafi is building a massive underground chemical weapons plant deep inside a mountain.

Sierra Nevada, Spain, 25
In the World Alpine Ski Championships, Italian skier Alberto Tomba wins the men's slalom. He had already won the giant slalom.

Berlin, 26
The Golden Bear for best film at the Berlin Film Festival is won by Taiwanese director Ang Lee's version of Jane Austen's *Sense and Sensibility*. It stars Emma Thompson, who also wrote the screenplay.

London, 26
The British government survives by one vote after a parliamentary debate on the Scott report into the arms-for-Iraq affair.

London, 26
An armed guard is put on Buckingham Palace as it is revealed that the British royal family is a target for the renewed IRA terrorist campaign.

New York, 27
Rupert Murdoch, head of Fox TV, says he will give free prime time slots to US presidential candidates during the month leading up to next November's election.

Englewood, CO, 27
US West Media Group announces it is taking over Continental Cablevision, an early result of the deregulation of the telecommunications industry.

London, 28
British prime minister John Major and Irish premier John Bruton agree on a timetable for the continuing Irish peace process. All-party talks on the future of Northern Ireland are set for June 10. (→ June 10)

Moscow, 29
President Boris Yeltsin of Russia and President Alexander Lukashenko of Belarus announce moves toward a greater integration of their two countries, both once part of the Soviet Union. (→ April 2)

CAPE CANAVERAL, MONDAY 26
Satellite breaks loose from space shuttle

A $442-million satellite was lost in space today when the 12-mile-long tether linking it to the space shuttle Columbia snapped. The tethered satellite was designed to generate electricity as the shuttle pulled it across the Earth's magnetic field. Researchers who had spent ten years developing the system were devastated by the setback.

The tethered satellite.

LONDON, WEDNESDAY 28
Princess Diana agrees to give Charles divorce

The front page of every British paper declares the long-awaited news of the royal divorce.

At a meeting in St. James's Palace today, the Princess of Wales agreed to Prince Charles's request for a divorce. The royal couple had been strongly urged to divorce by Queen Elizabeth II last December. At present, Diana would still become Queen if Charles succeeded to the throne.

A statement issued by the Princess said: "The Princess will continue to be involved in all decisions relating to the children and will remain at Kensington Palace." She will be known as "Diana Princess of Wales." The Queen said she was "most interested" by the announcement. (→ July 5)

LOS ANGELES, THURSDAY 29
Seal and Alanis scoop Grammys

The usually staid Grammy awards sprang surprises this evening. British singer Seal won three awards, including song of the year for "Kiss from a Rose." The other big winner was the Canadian singer-songwriter Alanis Morisette, whose four Grammys included album of the year for her provocative *Jagged Little Pill*.

Los Angeles, Sunday 25. Cambodian actor Haing Ngor (above right) was shot dead outside his home in the Chinatown area of Los Angeles. A refugee who survived captivity and torture under the Khmer Rouge, Ngor won an Oscar for his role in the movie *The Killing Fields*. Police have as yet no idea why he was killed.

Seal at the Grammy award ceremony.

UN denounces Cuba for downing two planes flown by Cuban exiles

The UN Security Council today issued a statement "strongly deploring" Cuba's shooting down of two unarmed planes. The UN condemnation falls far short of what Cuban-Americans feel is required. Tough new economic sanctions against Cuba announced by President Clinton yesterday have also failed to satisfy the exile community.

The unarmed Cessna 337s were shot down on Saturday by Cuban MiG fighters, just outside Cuban territorial waters. All four people on board are presumed dead. The aircraft were flown by pilots belonging to Brothers to the Rescue, a Cuban exile group founded by Jose Basulto. They were apparently looking for small boats and rafts attempting to cross the strait from Cuba to Florida.

President Clinton has described the downing of the two aircraft as "a flagrant violation of international law." New measures against Cuba will include tightening the US's economic blockade, as well as a block on tourist charter flights to the country from the US.

The anger of Cuban exiles at the downing of the aircraft has been partially diverted to a traitor from their own ranks. Juan Pablo Roque, formerly a prominent member of Brothers to the Rescue, appeared on Cuban television to denounce the exile organization as a CIA-backed group that repeatedly flew over Cuba expressly to note targets for sabotage.

President Fidel Castro faces up to new economic sanctions against his country.

Tombstone, Arizona, Tuesday 27. On the campaign trail for the Arizona primary, Republican presidential candidate Pat Buchanan poses as a gunslinger at the OK Corral. But the Buchanan bandwagon is faltering. In the primaries today, he only came third in Arizona and North Dakota, and second in South Dakota. (→ March 5)

(→ March 5)

Double suicide bombing in Israel kills 26

Terrorists have killed 26 people and injured more than 80 in two bomb attacks in Israeli cities today.

The worst incident occurred in Jerusalem, where a device carried by a suicide bomber exploded on board a commuter bus, killing 24 people and injuring more than 50. In the second attack, a terrorist drove a car bomb into a crowd of soldiers at a hitchhiking post in Ashkelon.

Hamas, the Islamic Resistance Movement, said it carried out the attacks to avenge the death of one of its members, Yahya Ayyash, in January.

The Israeli prime minister Shimon Peres was jeered when he visited the site of the bus bomb. Many Israelis view the peace process, to which Peres is committed, as exposing the country to terrorism.

Miami, Thursday 29. English golfer Nick Faldo spoke out today about his "month of hell" under the lash of the British tabloids. Last year the story broke that Faldo was leaving his wife and three children for 20-year-old Brenna Cepalak (above). Faldo recounts that he was under siege from journalists, with cameras trained on his house day and night. Now Faldo seems relaxed and ready to concentrate on his golf once more, in time for the US Masters. (→ April 14)

(→ April 14)

Gretzky is traded from the Kings to the Blues

Wayne Gretzky, the greatest hockey star of his generation, is on the move. The Los Angeles Kings yesterday traded Gretzky to the St. Louis Blues, picking up five young players in return.

Gretzky's future had been unclear since he told the Kings last month he did not want to stay with them. Blues president Jack Quinn said it was "a terrific day" for the St. Louis franchise.

Green guilty of Jordan murder

Jurors in Lumberton, North Carolina, have found 21-year-old Daniel Andre Green guilty of the killing of James R. Jordan, father of basketball star Michael Jordan. Green was convicted of first-degree murder, conspiracy, and first-degree robbery. Jordan was murdered in July 1993 as he slept in his car at the side of the road. (→ March 12)

(→ March 12)

San Jose, CA, 1
Researchers report that they have succeeded in transmitting a trillion bits of information a second through an optical fiber, equivalent to 12 million simultaneous phone calls.

Moscow, 1
Former Soviet president Mikhail Gorbachev says he will be a candidate in the Russian presidential election.

The Hague, 1
Serb general Djordje Djukic is indicted for war crimes by the Hague tribunal. (→ March 22)

Little Rock, 4
The Whitewater trial opens: on trial are Arkansas Governor Jim Guy Tucker and two former business associates of President Clinton, James and Susan McDougal. (→April 2)

Washington, DC, 4
A Supreme Court ruling allows police to confiscate a Michigan woman's car because her husband used it for sex with a prostitute.

Colorado, 5
Senator Bob Dole wins all eight Junior Tuesday primaries. Lamar Alexander and Senator Richard Lugar withdraw from the contest for the Republican nomination. (→March 7)

Weyauwega, WI, 5
A freight train derailment causes a propane tank to explode. The town of Weyauwega is evacuated because of the risk of further explosions.

Okinawa, 7
Three US servicemen found guilty of raping an Okinawan schoolgirl are sentenced by a Japanese court to prison terms of up to seven years.

New York, 7
Bob Dole wins convincingly in the New York primary. (→ March 12)

Geneva, 7
Swiss drug giants Sandoz and Ciba-Geigy merge to create Novaretis, the second biggest pharmaceuticals company in the world.

Deaths
March 9. George Burns, comedian, in Beverly Hills, at age 100.

Researchers succeed in cloning sheep

A perfect pair: Cloned sheep Megan and Morag at Edinburgh's Roslin Institute.

To most people, all sheep look alike. But Welsh mountain sheep Megan and Morag are more alike than others. They are clones—genetically identical animals produced by human ingenuity.

According to the journal *Nature*, researchers working at the Roslin Institute in Edinburgh took genetic material from a sheep embryo cell and placed it in an unfertilized ewe's egg from which the maternal genes were removed. The fertilized cells were then put into the wombs of ewes that acted as surrogate mothers. The result has been five cloned sheep, of which Megan and Morag survive.

The researchers believe they can now create thousands of mammal clones, including humans if desired. They will be able to "manufacture" animals with desirable traits.

TEL AVIV, TUESDAY 5

Israel stunned by festival bombing

Rescue workers on Dizengoff Street, the scene of Tel Aviv's shopping-mall bombing.

For the second time in two days, Palestinian suicide bombers have struck at the heart of Israel. On Sunday in Jerusalem a bus was blown up, killing 19 people. Today it was Tel Aviv's turn. A suicide bomber exploded a device outside a shopping mall crowded with families celebrating the festival of Purim. In a scene of unbearable carnage, 12 people were killed and 100 more injured. Some of the victims were children in fancy dress for the festival. The Islamic extremist organization Hamas has said it carried out both attacks.

Despite tough antiterrorist measures, the Israeli government seems incapable of stemming a wave of bombings that has cost 56 lives in nine days. But under pressure from the Palestinian leader Yassir Arafat, Hamas today called for a halt to the campaign.

TALLAHASSEE, FL, WED. 6

Top lawyer goes to jail

Prominent lawyer F. Lee Bailey has begun a six-month jail sentence for contempt of court. Bailey had failed to hand over to the government almost $22 million in cash and stock given him by a former client, Claude Duboc, a convicted drug trafficker. Bailey presented himself to the federal marshal's office in Tallahassee, Florida, this afternoon and was later led away in handcuffs. Bailey will be released once he pays up. (→ October 3)

NEW YORK, SATURDAY 9

Nelson replaced as Knicks coach

For the second straight season, basketball coach Don Nelson has lost his job. Last year he was ousted by the Golden State Warriors and joined the New York Knicks. Three times NBA Coach of the Year, he spoke of his burning ambition to win his first championship as coach.

But the Knicks fired Nelson today after a run of poor results and reports of differences with key players. Jeff Van Gundy, one of Nelson's assistant coaches, has taken over.

Los Angeles, Saturday 9. Robin Williams stars in *The Birdcage*, director Mike Nichols's version of the French drag movie *La Cage aux Folles*. *The Birdcage* is a hit despite its camp theme.

PONTIAC, MI, FRIDAY 8

Courts boost right-to-die campaign

Right-to-die campaigner Dr. Jack Kevorkian, acquitted in Michigan of assisted suicide.

In a landmark decision, a Court of Appeals in San Francisco has ruled in support of doctor-assisted suicide. The court struck down a Washington state law making assisted suicide a federal crime, and argued forcefully that there existed a constitutional right to die with dignity at a time of one's own choosing.

And in another notable verdict, a Michigan jury today acquitted Dr. Jack Kevorkian of assisted suicide, although he admitted helping two terminally ill people to inhale carbon monoxide. Dr. Kevorkian argued that he intended to relieve suffering, not to cause death. It was the second time he was acquitted under a Michigan law designed to stop his widely publicized actions. He declared the verdict "a tremendous stroke in favor of rationality."

CANBERRA, SUNDAY 3

Howard defeats Keating as Australia swings to the right

Australia ended 13 years of Labour government today as the Liberal-National coalition, led by John Howard, swept to victory in a general election. The coalition won a majority of more than 40 seats in the 148-seat House of Representatives.

The result means that Australia is unlikely to become a republic. Labour had wanted a president to replace Queen Elizabeth II as head of state.

Australian prime minister John Howard.

WASHINGTON, DC, FRIDAY 1

Networks agree to help parents censor TV viewing

Thirty top executives from the major US television networks met with President Clinton in the White House today to discuss the introduction of a ratings system for television programs. Ratings like those that are applied to movies will allow parents to identify shows that may be unsuitable for their children.

Agreed in principle by all the network heads, the system is to operate in combination with the V-chip, an electronic blocking device. This will be programmed to identify the rating attached to a show. Parents will be able to block access to material rated unsuitable for their child's age.

The networks say they hope to have agreed to details of the ratings system in time to put it into operation early next year.

Kuala Lumpur, Saturday 9. The PETRONAS towers, currently under construction in Malaysia's capital, are already the tallest buildings in the world. Reaching 1,482.61 ft above street level, the identical towers are 29 feet taller than the previous record-holder, Chicago's Sears Tower.

S	M	T	W	T	F	S
					1	2
3	4	5	6	7	8	9
10	11	12	13	14	15	16
17	18	19	20	21	22	23
24	25	26	27	28	29	30
31						

Johannesburg, 11
The trial opens of South African general Magnus Malan and 19 others accused of murder and conspiracy during the days of apartheid. (→ October 11)

Seoul, South Korea, 11
Two former presidents of South Korea, Chun Doo-hwan and Roh Tae-woo, go on trial charged with mutiny and treason for staging a coup in 1979 and ordering a massacre of protestors the following year. (→ August 26)

Montreal, 11
The Montreal Canadiens ice hockey team plays its last game in the 72-year-old Forum, one of the oldest sports arenas in North America.

Geneva, 12
The World Health Organization sets up an obesity task force to combat an epidemic of obesity worldwide.

Washington, DC, 12
President Clinton signs the Helms-Burton bill tightening the US economic embargo on Cuba.

Lumberton, NC, 12
Daniel Green is sentenced to life imprisonment for the murder of James Jordan, father of basketball star Michael Jordan.

New Orleans, 13
Leading cigarette company Liggett Group, involved in defending a class-action law suit over nicotine addiction, agrees to pay 5 percent of profits into quit-smoking programs.

Washington, DC, 14
Steve Forbes officially withdraws from the race for the Republican presidential nomination. (→ March 19)

Jerusalem, 14
After attending an antiterrorism summit in Egypt, President Clinton visits Israel and pledges $65 million to help Israel combat terrorist attacks.

Houston, TX, 16
A study conducted by researchers at the University of Houston suggests that 300 Mexicans die attempting to cross into the US every year.

US, TUESDAY 12

Bob Dole sweeps seven states as Perot gears up

Former presidential candidate Ross Perot addresses his Reform party supporters.

Senator Bob Dole is almost certain to be the Republican candidate in this year's presidential election after victories in all seven primaries on Super Tuesday. His wins included Texas and Florida, which between them send 221 delegates to the Republican convention. Dole has now secured more than 700 delegates, compared with around 70 for his remaining rivals Pat Buchanan and Steve Forbes. Two other Republican contestants, Lamar Alexander and Senator Richard Lugar, stepped down last week.

Steve Forbes is widely expected to announce his withdrawal from the race on Thursday. Despite spending millions on promotion, the maverick millionaire has won only two primaries, in Arizona and Delaware. Pat Buchanan has admitted that Dole's candidacy "appears inevitable," but he is determined to continue the contest.

Meanwhile, Ross Perot's Reform party is working in the wings to challenge President Clinton and senator Dole. Perot won 19 percent of the vote as an independent presidential candidate in the 1992 election. This time he says he does not intend to run himself. But with the president dogged by scandal and Dole lacking charisma, a Reform party candidate may well make a mark. (→ March 14)

DENVER, FRIDAY 15

Denver basketball player Abdul-Rauf reinstated

Nuggets point guard Mahmoud Abdul-Rauf, suspended for refusing to stand for the national anthem, has agreed to stand but pray at the same time. A convert to Islam who regards the US flag as "a symbol of oppression," Abdul-Rauf had been quietly sitting out the anthem all season, when two weeks ago his gesture became a public issue.

The controversial Mahmoud Abdul-Rauf.

Las Vegas, Saturday 16. Mike Tyson (right) becomes World Boxing Council heavyweight champion, defeating British titleholder Frank Bruno at the MGM Grand Garden arena. The fight was stopped 50 seconds into the third round of a one-sided contest. Bruno had held the title for 197 days.

DUNBLANE, WEDNESDAY 13

Massacre of the innocents at Dunblane

The massacred class of Dunblane Primary School: Teacher Gwenne Mayor (back row, left) and 16 of the children were killed; only one of the 29 children in the class escaped injury.

The worst multiple murder in modern British history brought horror and grief to the small Scottish town of Dunblane yesterday. A former Scout leader, Thomas Hamilton, shot dead 16 young children and a teacher in the local primary school before turning a gun upon himself.

The massacre happened just before 9:30 a.m. Hamilton walked into the school armed with four guns and forced his way into the gym, where a class of five- and six-year-olds were waiting to begin their exercises. The class's teacher, Gwenne Mayor, a part-time gym teacher, Eileen Harrild, and a supervisory assistant, Mary Blake, were in the room with the children.

Hamilton fired on the adults, killing Mrs. Mayor and wounding the two other adults. He then walked around the gym systematically shooting the children, killing 15 on the spot and fatally wounding one other. Only one child in the class escaped injury. After firing a volley into another classroom, fortunately hitting no one, Hamilton shot himself in the mouth.

Children's relatives outside Dunblane Primary School after the shooting.

Today the people of Dunblane are struggling to come to terms with the tragedy that has struck their quiet town. The headmaster of Dunblane Primary School, Ron Taylor, said: "Evil visited us yesterday and we don't know why. And we don't understand it and I guess we never will."

Thomas Hamilton was a local man, a loner with an interest in young boys and in guns. He seems to have been obsessed by his dismissal from the post of Scout leader in 1973. On the Friday before the killings, he wrote a letter to the Queen protesting against the damage the Scout Association had

Killer Thomas Hamilton.

done to his reputation; in another letter of complaint, he specifically mentioned Dunblane Primary School.

Although Hamilton was known to police because of complaints about his activities with boys' clubs, he had been issued firearms certificates for all his weapons. (→ October 16)

S	M	T	W	T	F	S
					1	2
3	4	5	6	7	8	9
10	11	12	13	14	15	16
17	18	19	20	21	22	23
24	25	26	27	28	29	30
31						

Chicago, 17
General Colin Powell tells the *Chicago Sun-Times* that he will not run for elective office. Senator Bob Dole hopes to persuade General Powell to run for vice-president.

Dedham, MA, 18
John Salvi III is found guilty of murdering two abortion clinic workers in December 1994.

Ohio, 19
Bob Dole sweeps the Mid-West primaries, effectively ensuring the Republican nomination.(→ March 26)

Michigan, 20
Storms and snow sweep Michigan and other states in the eastern US on the last day of winter.

Washington, DC, 20
Two protestors are arrested for disrupting a congressional hearing called to examine Louis Farrakhan's recent visit to Middle East and African countries.

Texas, 20
In a major setback for affirmative action, the Fifth US Circuit Court of Appeals rules that a University of Texas law school admission policy giving preference to blacks and Hispanics is unconstitutional.

London, 20
The British government announces the discovery of a possible link between a disease found in British cattle and a new strain of Creutzfeldt-Jakob disease in humans.

Milan, 20
Opera singer Luciano Pavarotti owns up to an affair with his 26-year-old secretary and says he is leaving his wife after 35 years of marriage.

Washington, DC, 21
The House of Representatives votes to allow public education to be denied to illegal immigrants.

The Hague, 22
The tribunal investigating war crimes in the former Yugoslavia makes its first indictment, of three Muslims and a Croat for the murder, torture, and rape of Serb prisoners.

Deaths
March 17. Rene Clement, French filmmaker, at age 82.

Taiwan defies China to elect president

Celebrating President Lee Teng-hui's victory in Taiwan; the election proceeded despite intimidation attempts by China.

Taiwan successfully held its first democratic presidential election today. The sitting president Lee Teng-hui scored a resounding victory with 54 percent of the vote, which was split between four candidates.

But the true victory was that the vote happened at all. It marks the end of four decades of single-party rule on the island. And it marks a triumph over intimidation from mainland China, which staged military maneuvers near Taiwan in the buildup to the election and threatened to invade the island if it declared its independence.

In China's view, Taiwan is a rebellious province that must one day be reunited with mainland China. President Lee pays lip service to "one China," although in practice he governs Taiwan as an independent state.

The US had sent two aircraft carriers to Taiwan to counter Chinese threats and this week agreed to sell the Taiwanese a range of high-tech military equipment.

SOUTH AFRICA, TUESDAY 19

Mandela speaks of his loneliness as divorce proceeds

Mandela: "I was the loneliest man."

South African president Nelson Mandela has been granted a divorce from his wife Winnie. The judge rejected Mrs. Mandela's argument that the president should submit to tribal mediation to save the marriage.

Yesterday, President Mandela told the court of the emptiness of his married life. "Ever since I returned from prison," he said, "not once has the defendant ever entered our bedroom whilst I was awake... I was the loneliest man during the period I spent with her." The president said he had been shown letters proving his wife's infidelity. Mrs. Mandela is claiming half of President Mandela's assets in settlement.

LOS ANGELES, FRIDAY 22

Jesse Jackson calls for Oscar boycott

The Reverend Jesse Jackson has called on television viewers to switch off next Monday's Academy Awards ceremony in protest at the lack of black nominees. Only one of the 166 nominees is an African American.

Jackson is mounting a prolonged campaign against what he alleges is endemic racism in the movie industry. His view is rejected, however, by many prominent black entertainment personalities. His boycott call is unlikely to be widely heeded, especially as this year's ceremony is being produced by Quincy Jones, who is black, and hosted by popular black star Whoopi Goldberg.

LOS ANGELES, WEDNESDAY 20

Menendez brothers found guilty in second trial

Lyle (left) and Erik Menendez—their first trial resulted in two hung juries.

Lyle and Erik Menendez were today found guilty of the shotgun killing of their parents after a second trial lasting five months. Their first trial in 1993-94 had ended with two juries failing to reach a verdict.

The brothers originally denied all responsibility for the murders, which took place in Beverly Hills in August 1989. They blamed the Mafia for the killings and went on a spending spree with their parents' $15 million fortune. After their arrest in March 1990, they confessed to the killings but claimed they were a consequence of sexual and psychological abuse by their father.

Despite undisputed evidence of a cold-blooded crime, Lyle's emotional performance in court persuaded some jurors to refuse to find them guilty of murder. This time Lyle did not testify and the jury brought a verdict of first-degree murder with special circumstances. This lays the Menendez brothers open to a possible death penalty. (→ April 17)

Manila, Philippines, Tuesday 19. At least 150 people were killed in a fire at the Ozone disco, Quezon City. Most were teenagers celebrating the start of school holidays. There was no fire exit and many were trampled to death in the rush to the only door.

DAYTON, OH, THURSDAY 21

Strike that closed General Motors ends

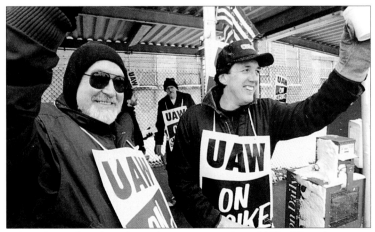

Striking GM workers: the strike cost the company an estimated $50 million a day.

A strike that had virtually closed down the largest industrial company in the US has ended. Two weeks ago 3,000 workers at GM's brake plants in Dayton, Ohio, walked out. By the middle of this week, 27 of GM's 29 assembly plants in the US, Canada, and Mexico were shut down for lack of parts. The company had laid off 177,000 workers and was losing an estimated $50 million a day.

The workers at the brake plants, members of the United Auto Workers labor union, were protesting the practice of "outsourcing"—buying parts from outside firms. They see this as a threat to their job security. Many US companies argue that outsourcing is essential, as union-negotiated benefits packages are increasingly making in-house workers uneconomical to employ.

CHICAGO, MONDAY 18

Rodman banned for six games

Chicago Bulls' $2.5-million-a-year star Dennis Rodman has been fined $20,000 and suspended for six games for headbutting official Ted Bernhardt after his ejection from a game in New Jersey on Saturday. It is the third-longest suspension in NBA history. "It's bad timing for us," said Michael Jordan. But the Bulls are still on target for a record-breaking season.

EDMONTON, CANADA, SAT. 23

US skaters win the top prizes

Michelle Kwan of the United States won the world figure skating championship at the Edmonton Coliseum tonight with a performance some observers described as the best ever by a woman on ice. Another US skater, Todd Eldredge, took the men's figure-skating title on Thursday. US champion Rudy Galindo came third behind Eldredge.

Paris, Tuesday 19. Michael Jackson and Saudi Prince al-Walid bin Talal, one of the world's richest investors, launch a show-business venture, Kingdom Entertainment, dedicated to "family values."

S	M	T	W	T	F	S
					1	2
3	4	5	6	7	8	9
10	11	12	13	14	15	16
17	18	19	20	21	22	23
24	25	26	27	28	29	30
31						

Washington, DC, 25
New $100 bills are delivered, the first major change in the design of the US currency since 1929.

Outer space, 25
Comet Hyakutake, the brightest comet in 20 years, reaches its closest point to the Earth and is clearly visible to the naked eye.

San Francisco, 25
In a mass ceremony 176 gay couples marry, as San Francisco grants lesbians and male homosexuals the right to city-sanctioned weddings.

Tuzla, 25
Hillary and Chelsea Clinton visit American peacekeepers in Bosnia.

Jordan, MT, 25
FBI agents arrest two leaders of the Freemen antigovernment group, LeRoy Schwietzer and Daniel E. Peterson, and lay siege to the Freemen ranch, known as Justus Township. (→ May 22)

California, 26
Bob Dole wins the Republican primaries in California, Washington state, and Nevada.

Cupertino, CA, 27
Apple Computer Inc. estimates its losses for the current quarter at around $700 million.

Dubai, United Arab Emirates, 27
US champion horse Cigar wins the Dubai World Cup, the world's most lucrative horse race.

Washington, DC, 28
Congress passes a bill banning controversial late-term abortions; President Clinton is expected to veto the bill.

Seattle, 31
The major league baseball season opens with the Seattle Mariners playing the Chicago White Sox. It is the earliest opening to the season in baseball history.

Deaths
March 26. Former senator Edmund S. Muskie, Democratic politician, in Washington, DC, at age 81.

March 26. David Packard, cofounder of Hewlett-Packard Inc., in Palo Alto, California, at age 83.

Oscars honor Scotland and a talking pig

Babe's visual effects team claims the only Oscar won by the film.

Christopher Reeve's appearance on stage was greeted by tears and an ovation.

Five-time nominee Susan Sarandon wins best actress for her role in Dead Man Walking.

Tartan set the pattern for this year's Academy Awards, with a triumph for Mel Gibson's kilted epic *Braveheart*, a boisterous movie loosely based on the life of thirteenth-century Scottish patriot William Wallace. *Braveheart* won five Oscars, including best picture, and best director for Gibson.

Susan Sarandon took the best actress award for her role as a nun in *Dead Man Walking*. It was the fifth time she had been nominated, but the first time she had won an award. The best actor award went to Nicolas Cage for his performance as an amoral suicidal alcoholic in *Leaving Las Vegas*, and Mira Sorvino won best supporting actress in *Mighty Aphrodite* as a dumb-blonde hooker.

Unfortunately not present at the award ceremony was Babe, the talking pig who wanted to be a sheepdog. One of the surprise movie successes of the last year, *Babe* won the award for best visual effects. Also absent was Oliver Stone, the director of *Nixon*, who had ostentatiously chosen to spend the evening with Zapatista guerrillas in Mexico.

The most moving moments of the evening were courageous appearances by *Superman* star Christopher Reeve, paralyzed in a riding accident last year, and Kirk Douglas, who recently suffered a stroke and struggled to deliver his speech accepting a special honorary award.

The Reverend Jesse Jackson led a small protest against the lack of black nominations for Academy Awards. Host Whoopi Goldberg made fun of Jackson's idea that blacks should wear rainbow ribbons in the ceremony as a sign of solidarity. The one black filmmaker nominated, Dianne Houston, lost.

Mel Gibson's Braveheart *swept the board, winning five Oscars, including best picture.*

TEL AVIV, WEDNESDAY 27
Israeli assassin is jailed for life

Jewish extremist Yigal Amir was sentenced to life imprisonment today for the assassination of Israeli prime minister Yitzhak Rabin. Amir killed Rabin in an attempt to stop the Palestinian peace process. He told the court: "Everything I did was for the God of Israel, the Torah of Israel, the people of Israel and the land of Israel." Judge Edmond Levy said Amir had "lost all semblance of humanity."

Rabin's assassin Yigal Amir remains unrepentant in the face of a life sentence.

Outer space, Monday 25. The Russian space station Mir and US space shuttle Atlantis fly together through space after docking yesterday. Today US astronaut Shannon Lucid floated through the shuttle to the space station where she will live for the next five months. "I am happy to be here," she stated.

CHINA, SUNDAY 31
China police raid orphans banquet

A charity banquet to raise funds for Chinese orphans was disrupted by plainclothes police tonight, throwing a further cloud over China's relations with the US. American novelist Amy Tan was to have been the keynote speaker at the event, which was attended by US businessmen and the US ambassador to China, Jim Sasser.

Police entered the hall before the dinner was under way, confiscated programs, and ripped down posters bearing the Chinese characters for "Love Children." They insisted that Ms. Tan not be allowed to make her speech.

Orphans have become a sensitive topic for the Chinese government, which has reacted angrily to accusations of mistreatment and neglect of children in state institutions.

GLEN CANYON, AZ, MONDAY 25
Artificial flood cleans up Colorado River

The flood's source: 117 billion gallons of water will be pumped through the canyon.

One of the boldest ecological experiments ever attempted began at dawn today. US interior secretary Bruce Babbitt pressed a button, pulled a lever, and turned a wheel to release a flood of water through the Glen Canyon dam into the Colorado River. Over the next week 117 billion gallons will surge through the Grand Canyon, imitating the regular spring floods that used to occur before the dam was built in 1963.

Scientists hope the artificial flood will cleanse and refresh the Colorado, reviving natural habitats and restoring the shoreline in the canyon. Some 200 observers will monitor the varying effects of the flood. "This is about restoring one of the most amazing, most beautiful places on Earth," Babbitt said. (→ October 9)

S	M	T	W	T	F	S
	1	2	3	4	5	6
7	8	9	10	11	12	13
14	15	16	17	18	19	20
21	22	23	24	25	26	27
28	29	30				

East Rutherford, NJ, 1
Kentucky Wildcats win the NCAA basketball championship, beating Syracuse 76–67.

Little Rock, 2
In the Whitewater trial, prosecution witness David Hale alleges that Bill Clinton, then governor, urged him to make an illegal loan. (→ April 28)

New York, 2
SBC Communications Inc. and Pacific Telesis Group agree to merge. They will form the second largest US telecommunications company.

Westminster, London, 2
Antiterrorist measures are rushed through the British parliament, giving police new powers to stop and search terrorist suspects.

New York, 3
A court of appeals rules that doctors in New York can assist suicide under certain circumstances.

Washington, DC, 3
A two-year study by the US Defense Department finds no evidence of "Gulf War syndrome" afflicting soldiers who took part in the conflict. (→ October 1)

Seoul, South Korea, 5
South Korean and US troops go on alert after North Korea announces it no longer recognizes the demilitarized zone separating it from the South since the Korean War. (→ April 16)

London, 5
Health authorities reveal that a test used to determine if people are HIV positive could be faulty. Some. 60,000 people declared clear of infection may not be.

British Columbia, Canada, 5
Estranged husband Mark Vijay Chahal kills nine people at his former wife's wedding party, including his former wife, before killing himself.

Zimbabwe, 6
Zimbabwean vice-president Joshua Nkomo announces publicly that his son has died of AIDS. He says the disease is "harvested by whites to obliterate blacks."

Deaths
April 6. Greer Garson, movie actress, at age 92, in Dallas.

CINCINNATI, MONDAY 1
Baseball opening shadowed by umpire's death

Baseball is sorely in need of good news after the troubles of recent seasons. But the headlines on the first full day of this year's program were filled with the death of one of the sport's most popular umpires, John McSherry, who collapsed shortly after the start of the Cincinnati Reds' season opener against the Montreal Expos. It is believed to be the first time a major-league umpire has died during a game.

Moscow, Tuesday 2. Russian president Boris Yeltsin (right) and president of Belarus Alexander Lukashenko (left) today signed an accord linking their economies and political systems. The alliance was blessed by Russian Orthodox patriarch Alexei II.

LINCOLN, MT, THURSDAY 4
Unabomber suspect arrested in Montana

In a one-room cabin 5 miles outside the small town of Lincoln, Montana, the FBI yesterday apprehended a man they firmly believe to be the Unabomber, responsible for 16 bomb attacks in the last 17 years.

Theodore J. Kaczynski, a Harvard graduate and former mathematics assistant professor at Berkeley, now a disheveled recluse, has been charged with the possession of bomb-related materials. A search of Kaczynski's cabin turned up a partially completed pipe bomb, sketches of explosive devices, and bomb-making materials. FBI agents are combing the tiny shack for evidence that links Kaczynski to the Unabomber outrages.

After one of the longest, most frustrating manhunts in the history of the FBI, the agency's attention was at last drawn to Kaczynski by his brother David. He tipped them off after spotting a similarity between papers his brother had written, found in the loft of their mother's former home in Illinois, and the published writings of the Unabomber.

The Unabomber's attacks had killed three people and injured 23. His main targets were universities, airlines, and computer stores. The individuals he killed were a computer store owner, an advertising executive, and the president of the California Forestry Association.

Last year the *Washington Post* agreed to publish a 35,000-word Unabomber manifesto denouncing the dehumanizing influences of modern society. (→ April 13)

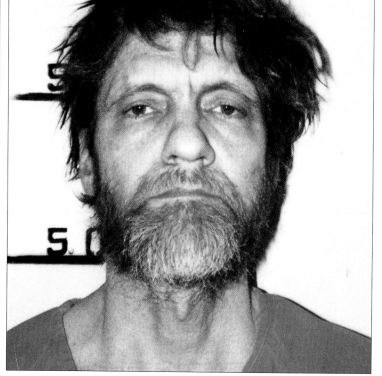

Suspect Theodore J. Kaczynski, arrested for possession of bomb-related materials.

The cabin where Kaczynski lived without electricity, running water, or a telephone.

Clinton grieves for air-crash victims

President Bill Clinton was at Dover Air Force Base, Delaware, today to mourn a friend who was also one of his closest political allies.

US Commerce Secretary Ronald H. Brown was among 33 people killed when their plane crashed into a mountainside near Dubrovnik in Croatia three days ago. The bodies were brought home to the US today in caskets ceremonially draped with the Stars and Stripes.

Ronald Brown was the first African American to be elected chairman of the Democratic National Committee and the first appointed to head the Commerce Department. He is credited with playing a major role in Clinton's election victory in 1992.

Brown was on a visit to Croatia and Bosnia to look for ways to back the rebuilding of the war-torn region.

President Clinton described Brown and his colleagues as "a stern rebuke to the cynicism that is all too familiar today." Visibly moved, the president said: "They believed in what they were doing. They believed in their country, and they believed they could make a difference." (→ April 12)

Ronald Brown during his visit in Tuzla.

President Clinton comforts Ronald Brown's widow as the caskets carrying the crash victims arrive at Dover Air Force base.

Birth-control jab for men unveiled

The World Health Organization today announced a breakthrough in birth control for men. An international team of scientists has developed and tested a weekly injection that reduces sperm production to a negligible level, while leaving sexual performance unimpaired.

Dr. Fred Wu of the University of Manchester, England, a member of the scientific team, said: "It is really for the first time showing the world that permanent contraception for men really works."

Schwarzkopf calls for ban on mines

General H. Norman Schwarzkopf, US commander in the Gulf War, is one of 15 retired generals and admirals who are urging the US to outlaw the use of land mines. In an open letter to President Clinton, published in the *New York Times*, they describe such a ban as "not only humane, but militarily responsible."

The US is currently operating a one-year moratorium on the use of land mines, but the Pentagon favors banning only "dumb" mines—those not designed to self-destruct after a certain time. Antimine campaigners estimate 26,000 people are killed or maimed by mines around the world every year. (→ May 16)

Britain caught in beef nightmare

Britain faces the prospect of slaughtering cattle on a massive scale in a desperate attempt to resolve the country's beef crisis.

Two weeks ago, the British government revealed a possible link between BSE, a disease found in some British cattle herds, and a new strain of the fatal Creutzfeld-Jakob disease in humans. The European Union imposed a worldwide ban on the export of British beef.

At first, the British government rejected calls for an immediate cull of millions of cattle. But the crisis would not go away. Today Britain failed to get the European export ban lifted, despite offering to kill and burn all cattle over 30 months old.

Europe is demanding more stringent measures, and even then will not promise to lift the export ban until confidence is restored. The British government is furious at European intransigence. Agriculture Minister Douglas Hogg said of the ban: "It is not justified. It is not based on scientific analysis." (→ May 21)

US Major League Soccer opens

In a fresh attempt to make soccer a big-money sport in the US, Major League Soccer (MLS) started its first season tonight in San Jose.

In front of a sell-out crowd, San Jose Clash beat Washington, DC, United 1-0, with a fine late goal from leading US goal scorer and World Cup star Eric Wynalda. "I don't think we could have scripted a better beginning," said chairman of the MLS, Alan Rothenberg.

Retired general Norman Schwarzkopf.

S	M	T	W	T	F	S
	1	2	3	4	5	6
7	8	9	10	11	12	13
14	15	16	17	18	19	20
21	22	23	24	25	26	27
28	29	30				

Peoria, IL, 9
A sexual harassment case is being brought by the Equal Employment Opportunities Commission against Mitsubishi in the US on behalf of female employees. It could be the biggest on record, worth $100 billion. (→ April 23)

Washington, DC, 9
A bill is signed giving the president power to reject specific items from the budget before signing it. Until now, the president could only accept or reject legislation in its entirety. (→ April 25)

Chicago, 9
The Chicago Bulls are beaten at home by the Charlotte Hornets, ending a 44-game home-winning streak.

Dusseldorf, Germany, 9
At least 16 people are killed and 150 injured after a fire breaks out in one of the terminals at Dusseldorf airport.

South Lebanon, 10
A Hizbollah mortar attack kills an Israeli soldier in south Lebanon. (→ April 13)

Washington, DC, 10
In a political corruption case, former congressman Dan Rostenkowski pleads guilty and is sentenced to 17 months in prison and fined $100,000.

Seoul, South Korea, 11
South Korean elections take away the government's majority in parliament. President Kim Young Sam's position is unthreatened, however.

Washington, DC, 12
Navy investigators blame pilot John Stacy Bates for the Navy F-14 Tomcat crash in Nashville in January. Bates and four others died in the crash.

Washington, DC, 12
Trade representative Mickey Kantor is named by Bill Clinton as commerce secretary to replace Ronald Brown.

Lincoln, MT, 13
Investigators claim to have discovered the original Unabomber manifesto in Theodore J. Kaczynski's cabin. (→ June 18)

Deaths
April 8. Ben Johnson, actor in classic Westerns, at age 77, in Mesa, Arizona.

Rusk, TX, Monday 8. Child molester Larry Don McQuay was released from jail under strict parole terms. He had requested castration, threatening otherwise to rape and kill children on his release.

BEIRUT, SATURDAY 13
Israelis attack targets in Lebanon

Israel has launched artillery and air strikes into Lebanon. Operation Grapes of Wrath is a response to rocket attacks by Hizbollah guerrillas targeting settlements in northern Israel from positions across the Lebanese border. As many as 60 Lebanese have been killed in the first three days of the Israeli operation, which began Thursday. (→ April 18)

MONROVIA, LIBERIA, THURSDAY 11
Westerners flee anarchy in strife-torn Liberia

US helicopters are ferrying Americans and other foreign nationals to safety as the West African state of Liberia once more descends into chaos.

Armed supporters of Liberian warlord Roosevelt Johnson went on the rampage in Monrovia after he was dismissed from the government and the Council of State ordered his arrest for murder. Members of the West African peacekeeping force, installed in Liberia at the end of a previous civil conflict, have reportedly joined in the looting.

Hundreds of foreign nationals have taken refuge in the US embassy compound, but many others are cut off in other parts of the country. A US naval force in the Mediterranean is being diverted to Liberia. (→ May 14)

Fighters in the Liberian conflict; Monrovia was described as a "frenzy of looting."

LOS ANGELES, FRIDAY 12
Brando stirs controversy with comments on Jews

Marlon Brando (right), being interviewed last week on Larry King Live.

Actor Marlon Brando has been denounced by the Jewish Defense League for comments he made as a guest on CNN's *Larry King Live.* Brando launched an extremely outspoken denunciation of racism in Hollywood movies and appeared to blame Jews in the film industry for the racial prejudice. Brando said that Hollywood had presented every offensive racial stereotype but "never the kike because they knew that's where you draw the wagons around."

Brando claimed his remarks had been taken out of context. Today he visited Rabbi Marvin Hier, founder of the Museum of Tolerance in Los Angeles, in a gesture of conciliation. Rabbi Hier said he was convinced Brando was not an antisemite.

CHEYENNE, WY, THURSDAY 11
Child pilot killed in record attempt

Seven-year-old Jessica Dubroff in her Cessna shortly before the crash.

A seven-year-old girl may have been at the controls when a single-engine Cessna crashed today in driving rain and snow. Jessica Dubroff was killed along with her father, Lloyd, and her flight instructor, Joe Reid.

Jessica was attempting to become the youngest person to fly across the US coast-to-coast and back. Her aircraft had just taken off from Cheyenne Municipal Airport on the second leg of the journey when it ran into trouble. It crashed into the driveway of a house in a residential area of city. "There was a last attempt by the pilot not to hit houses," said local police chief John Powell.

A child is not allowed a pilot's license, but an instructor can let a child operate the controls. Mitch Barker, an aviation administration spokesman, said that Jessica Dubroff was "considered to be a passenger. The instructor is considered in control of the aircraft."

MIAMI, FRIDAY 12
Manatees struck by mystery disease

Florida's best-loved animal, the manatee, or sea cow, is under threat. A mystery epidemic has killed 221 manatees so far this year, 120 of them in the last month. The previous record for manatee deaths was 206 in 1990. Scientists are struggling to understand the disease and save the animals—with this death rate they will be wiped out in two years. (→ July 3)

The endangered Florida manatee.

CHICAGO, WEDNESDAY 10
Tyson denies harassment allegation

LaDonna August, a beautician from Gary, Indiana, has accused boxing champion Mike Tyson of assault. The alleged incident occurred at The Clique, a Chicago nightclub. According to Ms. August, Tyson—who is still on parole after serving three years in jail for rape—touched her and bit her on the cheek. Tyson denies the allegations. (→ October 24)

Beautician LaDonna August.

Los Angeles, Saturday 13. Japanese pitcher Hideo Nomo of the Los Angeles Dodgers pitched a three-hitter and struck out 17 batters in a 3-1 victory over the Florida Marlins here tonight. The Dodgers are currently fielding five starting pitchers from five different countries—South Korea, Japan, the Dominican Republic, Mexico, and the US—an example of the increasing internationalization of the sport.

April

Boston, 15
Kenyan Moses Tanui wins the 100th Boston Marathon; Uta Pippig from Germany wins the women's race.

Moscow, 15
Trojan gold seized by Soviet troops from Berlin in 1945 goes on display in Moscow amid German demands for the treasures to be returned.

East London, South Africa, 15
The Truth and Reconciliation Commission, chaired by Archbishop Desmond Tutu, opens in South Africa, to look into the crimes of apartheid. (→ August 21)

Seoul, South Korea, 16
President Clinton, on his visit to South Korea, proposes four-nation peace talks involving North and South Korea, China, and the US.

Miami, 16
The mother of a repeatedly ill child, Jennifer Bush, used as an example by President Clinton to show the failings of the health-care system, is arrested for deliberately poisoning her child.

London, 16
Madonna's publicist tells Britain's GMTV that the pop star is four months pregnant; the father is Carlos Leon, a Cuban fitness instructor. (→ October 15)

Manila, 17
The Philippines bans the export of live monkeys after two Philippine monkeys die in a breeding facility in Texas from an Ebola-like virus.

Milwaukee, WI, 17
The Chicago Bulls make basketball history by winning their seventieth game of the season, with three games still left to play. (→ April 21)

Los Angeles, 17
The jury in the Menendez brothers trial recommends life imprisonment for the two young men convicted of killing their parents.

Cairo, 18
Islamic terrorists kill 18 Greek tourists in a shooting attack near the pyramids.

Deaths
April 15. Stavros Niarchos, Greek shipping magnate, in Zurich, Switzerland, at age 86.

LAHORE, PAKISTAN, SUN. 14
Cancer hospital devastated by bomb blast

The hospital's founder, Imran Khan.

A bomb exploded in the Shaukat Khanum cancer hospital, Lahore, today, killing six people. The hospital was founded by former Pakistani sport star Imran Khan, a friend of Princess Diana and a critic of the Pakistan government. The bombing was probably politically motivated. An angry Khan said: "It was the work of a savage or an animal because human beings cannot do such a thing to a hospital."

OKLAHOMA CITY, FRIDAY 19
Marking the Oklahoma tragedy

At 9:02 a.m., thousands of people stood in silence at the site of the Alfred P. Murrah federal building in Oklahoma City, where exactly one year ago a massive bomb explosion killed 168 people in the worst act of terrorism ever committed on US soil.

The 168 seconds' silence (one second for each victim) was observed by people across the US, including Congress in Washington and the New York stock exchange. Afterward, relatives of the victims came forward to leave mementos on the site. (→ July 15)

Mourners attach mementos to the fence surrounding the federal building compound.

AUGUSTA, GA, SUNDAY 14
Norman collapse gives Masters to Faldo

Australian golfer Greg Norman, the highest-ranked player in the world, threw away a six-shot lead to lose the US Masters tournament today. After one of the most humiliating collapses in golfing history, Norman ended five strokes behind Britain's Nick Faldo.

Playing with a predatory arrogance to match his nickname, the Great White Shark had dominated the first three rounds of the tournament. He entered the last day needing only a steady performance to win easily.

But kept under constant pressure by Faldo's faultless play, Norman's confidence fell apart. The crowd was hushed as mistake followed mistake. On the final green, a comfortable winner, Faldo attempted to console a distraught Norman with a hug.

"It was an amazing day," Faldo, who had won his third Masters, said afterward. "I honestly and genuinely feel sorry for Greg." Norman put a brave face on his disaster: "Nick played great and I played poor. There were no two ways about it."

Nick Faldo hugs Greg Norman (left) as they finish the eighteenth hole of the Masters.

BRAZIL, FRIDAY 19

Cave finds alter view of prehistory

According to the journal *Science*, rock paintings and stone weapons found in a cave near the Amazon River show a previously unknown culture existing in the Americas 11,000 years ago.

Previously it was thought all Native Americans descended from a single wave of big-game hunters who migrated from Siberia down through the Americas. But the cave materials suggest there was an earlier migration of quite different peoples.

London, Wednesday 17. Plans were unveiled for a 500-ft Ferris wheel to be built in the center of London as part of the millennium celebrations. Situated on the south bank of the Thames, the wheel will be almost twice the height of Big Ben opposite.

LONDON, WEDNESDAY 17

Royal divorce is a friendly affair

The Duke and Duchess of York, the son and daughter-in-law of Queen Elizabeth II, were granted a "quickie" divorce in the Family Division of the High Court in London today. The couple were married in Westminster Abbey in July 1986 and have been separated for more than two years. The divorce will become final, or "absolute," in six weeks' time.

The Duchess, popularly known as "Fergie," said today that she and her ex-husband remained "the bestest of friends." The divorce settlement of $3 million is mostly held in trust for the royal children. Fergie will have about $750,000 for herself, not nearly enough to cover her alleged debts in excess of $4.5 million. (→ May 30)

BEIRUT, THURSDAY 18

Israeli "mistake" is tragedy for Lebanese

A UN base near Tyre in southern Lebanon was pounded by Israeli artillery today, killing 100 people, mostly women and children. The base was crowded with Lebanese civilians who had taken refuge there to escape the Israeli bombardment of their villages. An estimated 400,000 Lebanese have fled their homes since Israel began hitting southern Lebanon eight days ago, in response to rocket attacks on Israel by Hizbollah guerrillas.

UN paramedics carry away the wounded; 100 people were killed in the bombardment.

The scene of carnage at the UN base was witnessed by Hassan Seklawi, a Lebanese working with the UN: "My white rubber shoes have turned red from the blood," he said. "I had to walk over bodies that covered the walkways at the base."

Israeli foreign minister Ehud Barak called the bombardment of the UN base an unfortunate mistake. "The actual shooting was done by our forces, but the overall responsibility lies with Hizbollah and the government of Lebanon," he said. The Israelis claim they were responding to fire from Hizbollah guerrillas positioned a few hundred yards from the UN base.

President Clinton called for an immediate cease-fire, and announced he is sending Secretary of State Warren Christopher to the region to try to further negotiations. Israeli prime minister Shimon Peres has refused to proclaim a cease-fire, however, saying that the assault will continue until Hizbollah stops its attacks on settlements in northern Israel. (→ April 26)

TOKYO, THURSDAY 18

US and Japan strengthen their alliance

In a three-day official visit to Japan, President Clinton has sought to confirm the US-Japanese alliance as the key to security in East Asia. Recent saber-rattling by China and North Korea has emphasized the continuing threat of conflict in the region.

On Wednesday President Clinton and Japanese Prime Minister Ryutaro Hashimoto signed a declaration— Alliance of the 21st Century—pledging US troops to stay in Asia beyond the millennium, and committing Japan to a more active role in regional defense in support of US forces.

The presence of 47,000 US troops in Japan is highly controversial, especially since the rape of a 12-year-old Okinawan girl by three US servicemen last year. President Clinton publicly apologized for the rape in his speech to the Japanese parliament. To help defuse criticism, the US has agreed to return 20 percent of the land it holds in Okinawa, but it is not reducing the number of US troops stationed there, currently 29,000.

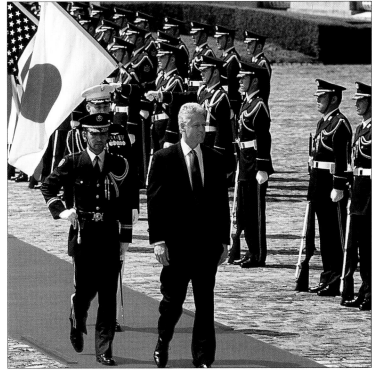

The president's trip to Japan is seen as the most important US-Japan summit for decades.

April

MARYLAND, MONDAY 29
Former CIA director Colby goes missing

William J. Colby, the director of the CIA from 1973 to 1976, has been missing since Sunday. His canoe was found capsized close to his vacation home in Rock Point, Maryland. Coast Guard crews are now searching the Wicomico River.

Colby, age 76, was the top US intelligence officer in Saigon during the Vietnam War. Currently, foul play is not suspected. (→ May 6)

WASHINGTON, DC, SUNDAY 28
Washington's mayor takes a rest cure

Washington Mayor Marion Barry feels he needs a break for "spiritual rejuvenation."

Marion Barry, the controversial mayor of Washington, DC, has announced that he is taking a week off work in a search for "physical, mental, and spiritual rejuvenation." He intends to spend the week at the Skinner Farm Leadership Institute, at Tracys Landing in rural Maryland.

Given Mayor Barry's previous conviction on a drugs charge, there was bound to be speculation that he had relapsed into drug and alcohol abuse. He vigorously denies such allegations, however, and says that he has no plans to resign from his job. (→ May 13)

PORT AUTHUR, TASMANIA, MONDAY 29
Gunman kills 34 in Tasmanian massacre

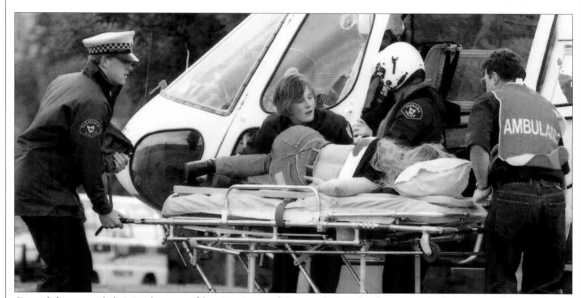

Rescue helicopters rush the injured—many of them in serious condition—to the Royal Hobart Hospital, which was on full disaster alert.

After a siege lasting 16 hours, police this morning arrested 28-year-old Martin Bryant for the massacre of at least 34 people at Port Arthur, a popular tourist site on the Australian island of Tasmania.

The carnage began on Sunday afternoon when the gunman pulled an automatic rifle out of a tennis bag in the Broad Arrow cafeteria and opened fire at random. The cafeteria was packed with tourists, most of them Australians. Twenty people died there. Over the next 30 minutes the gunman roamed the area, killing at will. He seized a car, shooting dead the four occupants. He pursued and killed a six-year-old girl after murdering her mother and her three-year-old sister. Finally the gunman took three hostages in the Seascape guest house, where he was besieged by police. Early this morning he set fire to the building and ran out with his clothes ablaze. Suffering from burns, he was taken to the same hospital as many of the victims he had shot.

First reports allege that Bryant has known psychological problems. It may not be the first time he has killed. His father was believed to have shot himself, but police are now reopening the case. Helen Harvey, an elderly woman who acted as his benefactor, died in a car crash with Bryant at the wheel. (→ September 30)

Police say Martin Bryant, age 28, has a history of psychological problems.

NEW YORK, MONDAY 29

Bidding fever for Kennedy relics

JFK's favorite rocking chair is sold at Sothebys for $400,000—more than 100 times the estimated preauction price.

A bidder displays her piece of Camelot.

Asked to auction a range of Jackie Kennedy Onassis's personal possessions, Sotheby's estimated their overall value at $4.6 million. The auctioneers had failed to understand the US's continuing love affair with Jackie and John F. Kennedy. Today, after four days of fevered bidding, the sale had realized a grand total of $34.5 million.

Winning bids included $400,000 for JFK's favorite rocking chair, estimated price $3,000, and $574,500 for the president's cigar humidor. A triple strand of fake pearls, a kind that can be bought in department stores for around $30, sold for $211,500. Actor Arnold Schwarzenegger, who is married to JFK's niece, paid $772,500 for a set of the president's golf clubs.

Jackie Onassis apparently planned the sale before her death in 1994. The proceeds will benefit her children. Before the auction the Kennedy children donated 38,000 photographs and manuscripts to the JFK Library and Museum in Boston.

CHICAGO, TUESDAY 23

Sex-harassment lawsuit protest

Workers from the Mitsubishi auto plant in Normal, Illinois, protested in Chicago today against the sexual harassment suit being brought against the company by the Equal Employment Opportunity Commission. Critics of the company pointed out that the workers had been bused to the demonstration by Mitsubishi, and paid their wages for the day.

The lawsuit is based on complaints filed by 29 women at the Mitsubishi plant between 1992 and 1994. The allegations of harassment range from verbal abuse to unwanted physical contact and pressure to grant sexual favors. It is potentially the largest sexual harassment case ever brought. The women are also pursuing a civil suit against Mitsubishi. (→ May 8)

TOKYO, WEDNESDAY 24

Trial of Japanese cult leader Asahara opens

Cult leader Shoko Asahara went on trial today for ordering last year's nerve gas attack on the Tokyo subway that killed 11 and injured thousands.

Appearing before the judges in a blue prison uniform and handcuffs, Asahara refused to enter a plea, and rejected the use of his real name, Chizuo Matsumoto. He sat with his eyes closed during the proceedings.

Asahara's Aum Shinrikyo sect once numbered 10,000. He could be hanged if convicted of the murder charges facing him.

Cult leader Shoko Asahara, age 41.

LOS ANGELES, WEDNESDAY 24

Superman actress in "mental distress"

Margot Kidder, the Canadian actress who played Lois Lane in the *Superman* movies, is under observation in a Los Angeles hospital after being found dazed and confused in the backyard of a house in the suburb of Glendale.

Ms. Kidder, age 47, disappeared on Saturday evening from Los Angeles International Airport. When found, she appeared to have lost two teeth, had cut off her own hair with a razor, and, according to a Glendale police officer, was in "obvious mental distress." Ms. Kidder had recently been making a comeback from serious injury and bankruptcy.

Superman star Margot Kidder.

SAN FRANCISCO, FRIDAY 26

Six-year-old on attempted murder charge

In Richmond, a suburb of San Francisco, a six-year-old boy has been arrested for the savage beating of a newborn baby. The boy allegedly broke into a neighbor's house with two of his friends, tipped 34-day-old Ignacio Bermudez Jr. out of his bassinet, and kicked and clubbed him until he was near death. The six-year-old is believed to be the youngest person ever charged with attempted murder in the US.

May

S	M	T	W	T	F	S
			1	2	3	4
5	6	7	8	9	10	11
12	13	14	15	16	17	18
19	20	21	22	23	24	25
26	27	28	29	30	31	

Detroit, 1
A second-degree murder verdict is delivered in the trial of Martell Welch, who drove a woman to drown herself by chasing her through a public park while at least 40 people watched and failed to intervene.

New York, 1
Rent, a musical about drugs and AIDS on New York's Lower East Side, sells out on Broadway. (→ June 2)

Ardmore, PA, 2
Kobe Bryant, a 17-year-old top high-school basketball player, chooses to move straight to the NBA without attending college.

Washington, DC, 2
US agents make arrests across the country, claiming to have broken a Mexican-Colombian cocaine ring.

Louisville, KY, 4
Grindstone, ridden by Jerry Bailey, wins the 122nd Kentucky Derby over Cavonnier in a photo finish.

Madrid, 4
Jose Maria Aznar becomes the new conservative prime minister of Spain after a coalition deal is achieved.

Moscow, 6
Russia announces it is to expel several British diplomats for espionage.

Rock Point, MD, 6
Former CIA chief William Colby's body is found on a riverbank, more than a week after he disappeared while canoeing.

The Hague, Netherlands, 7
The Bosnian War Crimes Tribunal opens, with Texan Gabrielle Kirk McDonald chairing the panel of judges.

Germany, 8
Antinuclear demonstrators trying to halt the dumping of nuclear waste clash with 15,000 police in Germany.

India, 8
The corruption-racked governing Congress party is routed in Indian elections that leave no party with a clear mandate to govern. (→ May 16)

Washington, DC, 8
Jesse Jackson and the National Organization of Women are urging a boycott of Mitsubishi products over the company's handling of sexual harassment allegations. (→ May 14)

London, Wednesday 8. A new portrait of Queen Elizabeth II was unveiled today by artist Antony Williams (above). Critics said it made the Queen look old and worn; the artist called it a fair portrait of a 70-year-old.

WASHINGTON, DC, MONDAY 6
A round of golf with Clinton nets $76,000

A Washington civil servant, Robert Peck, has bid $76,000 for the chance to play an 18-hole round of golf with President Clinton. The president had offered the round for auction as his contribution to annual fund-raising for Chelsea Clinton's private school, Sidwell Friends.

Robert Peck, manager of computer systems for the US Customs Service, said the school was "worth supporting." The president's political opponents have denounced the auction as improper, although there is no suggestion he will benefit personally.

President Clinton waves to the cameras during a golfing trip in Florida.

FLORIDA, SATURDAY 11
Valujet flight 592 crashes in the Everglades

A DC-9 airliner flying from Miami to Atlanta has crashed in the Florida Everglades. The disintegrated wreckage of the aircraft has been swallowed up by the swamp. None of the 109 people on board can have survived.

The pilot of Valujet flight 592, Captain Candalyn Kubeck, radioed air traffic control shortly after takeoff from Miami International Airport to report smoke in the cockpit. The aircraft turned back but crashed in the swamp 15 miles from Miami. Investigators face an awesome task as they scour the swamp for evidence of the cause of the crash. Guards have been set to protect workers from alligators and poisonous snakes.

Valujet is a low-fare airline based in Atlanta. Like other discount airlines, it has benefitted from changes in airline regulations in recent years. Critics argue that safety standards have been lowered to cut costs. Valujet is already the subject of a safety review by the Federal Aviation Administration because of earlier incidents. (→ May 16)

MINNESOTA, SATURDAY 11
Bear hunt is controversial dying wish

A Minnesota teenager dying of a brain tumor is to be granted his last wish—to hunt and kill a Kodiak bear. The boy, whose full name has been withheld, is a beneficiary of the Make-A-Wish Foundation, which regularly tries to fulfill the last requests of terminally ill children. He is to be sent to Alaska, provided with a Magnum rifle, and given the services of a taxidermist should he succeed.

Fulfillment of the wish has been opposed by animal-rights groups and has also split the Make-A-Wish-Foundation itself. But the foundation's president, James E. Gordon, said the wishes it granted were "limited only by the child's imagination."

US, Friday 10. *Twister* takes the US box office by storm, grossing $37.5 million in its first weekend. Directed by *Speed*'s Jan De Bont and starring Helen Hunt and Bill Paxton, *Twister* was heavily hyped in advance for its state-of-the-art, computer-generated effects.

NEW YORK, SATURDAY 4
Dole campaign leader calls Buchanan divisive

At the moment, Republicans often seem more interested in attacking one another than in hitting President Clinton. Senator Alfonse D'Amato, chairman of the steering committee for Senator Bob Dole's presidential campaign, stirred up feeling today with an outspoken attack on Pat Buchanan and the Republican right-wing.

While appealing for tolerance of different views within the party, D'Amato derided Buchanan as a "philosophical ayatollah" and called his campaign divisive. "Pat Buchanan is bashing women and belittling them," D'Amato said, "and African Americans and Jews and gays. That's not the message of inclusiveness."

Senator Alfonse D'Amato.

NORTH CAROLINA, WED. 8
Gantt takes on Helms in rematch

Harvey Gantt, former mayor of Charlotte, is to attempt to unseat Republican Senator Jesse Helms in this year's elections in North Carolina. Gantt won the Democratic nomination, despite suggestions that, as an African American, he could not hope to defeat Helms in the predominantly white-voter state.

Gantt lost to Helms in 1990, but he says of himself now: "I'm six years older, I'm six years wiser, I'm six years grayer, and I'm six years tougher."

Western US, May. The Olympic flame is making its way across the US from Los Angeles to Atlanta. The route was planned so that 90 percent of the population would be able to see it without having to drive for more than two hours. On May 8 in Washington the flame was briefly extinguished when the cyclist carrying the torch fell—but it was swiftly reignited using what organizers called the "mother flame."

CAPE TOWN, THURSDAY 9
De Klerk's Nationalist party deserts Mandela's coalition government

F.W. de Klerk told South Africa he is "raring to go as leader of the opposition."

F.W. de Klerk announced today that his Nationalist party is to withdraw from South Africa's coalition government and go into opposition. It was the surprising alliance between de Klerk's white-supremacist Nationalists and Nelson Mandela's ANC that led South Africa out of apartheid. The break-up of the coalition seems sure to increase instability. The value of the rand fell sharply at the news, which comes a day after the South African national assembly agreed a new multiracial constitution.

COLUMBUS, OH, THURSDAY 9
Byrd diary reveals the truth of polar flight

Seventy years after US aviator Richard Byrd claimed to have become the first person to fly to the North Pole, the truth concerning this much-contested event seems to have come to light. Those claiming Byrd was a fake who never even made an attempt to fly to the Pole are wrong—but although he tried, he never got there.

Researcher Dennis Rawlins was asked by Ohio State University to examine the diary Byrd kept on the flight. Rawlins reports that careful analysis shows Byrd flew to within about 150 miles of the Pole before turning back. Byrd later lied about the flight, claiming he circled the Pole several times. But at least, comments Rawlins, Byrd did carry out a hazardous flight into the unknown, which should restore his "reputation for courage and ability." The first true Polar flight is now attributable to Norwegian Roald Amundsen.

May

S	M	T	W	T	F	S
			1	2	3	4
5	6	7	8	9	10	11
12	13	14	15	16	17	18
19	20	21	22	23	24	25
26	27	28	29	30	31	

Wilmington, DE, 13
Laura Davies overcomes winds and cold weather to win the McDonald's LPGA Golf Championship.

New Orleans, 13
Tulane Medical School research finds that women suffer greater damage from smoking than men do due to the smaller size of their lungs.

Bangladesh, 13
A tornado levels 80 Bangladeshi villages, killing at least 508 people. More than 500 people are still missing.

Washington, DC, 13
Mayor Marion Barry returns from a two-week retreat, rejecting claims he was back on drugs and alcohol.

Chicago, 14
Mitsubishi announces it is hiring former Labor Secretary Lynn Martin to investigate its policies and practices in response to sexual harassment accusations.

New York, 14
Dwight Gooden pitches a no-hitter for the New York Yankees against Seattle after his return from suspension for substance abuse.

New Brunswick, NJ, 16
Fourteen-year-old Hannes Sarkuni graduates from Rutgers University with a degree in computer science and math. He enrolled in Rutgers two years ago, straight from eighth grade.

Washington, DC, 16
President Clinton announces a limited ban on land mines, following a UN agreement last week, and instructs the military to begin destruction of four million antipersonnel mines.

Liverpool, England, 16
British TV broadcasts film footage of the Beatles, taken three years before they became famous. The color film, which has no soundtrack, was found in a drawer in a house in Liverpool.

Baltimore, 18
The 121st Preakness is won by Louis Quatorze, ridden by Pat Day and trained by Nick Zito.

Deaths
May 17. Racing driver Scott Brayton is killed, at age 37, during practice for the Indianapolis 500.

Dole gambles all on the presidency

Bob Dole—his dramatic announcement may kick start a stalled presidential campaign.

Senator Bob Dole, now certain of nomination as Republican candidate for the presidency, announced today that he is to give up the Senate seat he has held for 27 years to concentrate fully on the presidential contest. In an emotional statement Senator Dole said: "I will seek the presidency with nothing to fall back on but the judgment of the people, and nowhere to go but the White House or home."

The announcement has stunned Washington. Some top Republicans thought Senator Dole would give up his title as majority leader, but no one had expected him to leave the Senate.

Ghana, Tuesday 14. Nearly 4,000 Liberians were granted haven here today when authorities allowed the ship Bulk Challenge to dock. In what was called "the voyage of the damned," the refugees on the ill-equipped, overcrowded ship had been seeking asylum for ten days.

Hostages freed after four-month jungle ordeal

Nine hostages, including four Britons and two Dutch, were freed when Indonesian troops attacked a rebel camp in the jungle of Irian Jaya yesterday. The nine had been held hostage since January.

Six rebels and two hostages died during the rescue. The rebels belong to the Free Papua Movement, which is seeking independence for Irian Jaya from Indonesian rule.

Washington, DC, Thursday 16. A team of paleontologists today announced the discovery in Morocco of a skull 5 ft high. The find confirms the past existence of *Carcharodontosaurus saharicus* (shark-toothed reptile from the Sahara), a carnivore bigger than *Tyrannosaurus rex*.

Reeve upbeat on recovery from paralysis

Actor Christopher Reeve, paralyzed by a riding accident a year ago, is fighting for recovery in the only way he can—by lobbying for funds for research into spinal cord injuries.

Today Reeve went to the White House and won a promise of $10 million research funding from President Clinton. He asked Congress to come up with another $30 million. The actor is determined to walk again. He insists that on his fiftieth birthday, in 2002, he will "stand up and toast everyone at the party."

MOSCOW, THURSDAY 16
Yeltsin bids for Russian votes

Russian president Boris Yeltsin is showering voters with promises in the run-up to next month's elections. Today he pledged to abolish the deeply unpopular compulsory military service by the year 2000, and to pay compensation to senior citizens cheated of money in investment frauds—the first payment timed for six days before the election. Yeltsin also promised to phase out the death penalty, a requirement for joining the Council of Europe.(→ June 17)

NEW DELHI, THURSDAY 16
India in confusion as new PM moves in

Prime Minister Atal Bihari Vajpayee.

The collapse of the corruption-racked Congress party in last week's Indian elections has left the world's second most populous nation in a state of uncertainty and confusion. Congress had dominated Indian political life since independence.

Today, with no group commanding a majority, Atal Bihari Vajpayee, head of the Hindu Bharatiya Janata Party (BJP), was sworn in as prime minister. His chances of governing effectively look slim, however. The BJP won less than 25 percent of the popular vote.(→ May 28)

MIAMI, THURSDAY 16
Valujet crash raises questions

The salvage site of the Valujet crash.

As investigators continue the arduous operation of searching the Everglades swamp for fragments of Valujet Flight 592, which crashed there last Saturday, a theory has begun to emerge of a possible cause for the disaster. About 50 oxygen canisters, officially classified as hazardous cargo, were being carried under the aircraft's main cabin. They had been wrongly labeled as empty.

Valujet's safety record, and that of other economy airlines, is coming under hostile scrutiny. The inspector general at the Transportation Department, Mary Schiavo, has questioned assurances from the Federal Aviation Authority (FAA) that Valujet is a safe airline. "You can pass the exam with a C or you can pass the exam with an A," she commented.

The FAA is appointing hundreds of extra inspectors, and President Clinton has ordered the Transportation Department "to ensure all our airlines continue to operate at the highest level of safety." (→ May 19)

WASHINGTON, DC, THURS. 16
Top US admiral shoots himself

Admiral Jeremy Boorda, the US Chief of Naval Operations, was found dead today outside his quarters at the Washington Navy Yard. He had shot himself in the chest with a .38 pistol.

Admiral Boorda, age 57, was known to be distressed by the imminent disclosure in the press that he had improperly worn two decorations for valor to which he had no right. The admiral described the wearing of the valor decorations as an honest mistake, but apparently felt that his explanation would not be believed.

President Clinton described Admiral Boorda as a man of "extraordinary dedication and good humor."

Admiral Jeremy Boorda.

KATHMANDU, TUESDAY 14
Death and heroism as storm sweeps Everest

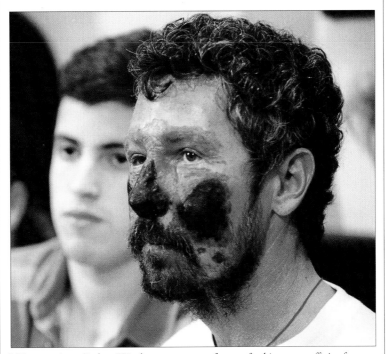
US mountaineer Seaborn Weathers, at a press conference after his rescue, suffering from severe windburn on his face and badly frostbitten hands.

About 30 climbers were attempting to scale Mount Everest, the world's tallest peak, last weekend when a blizzard struck. One US mountaineer was rescued yesterday by helicopter, but eight other climbers are still missing, presumed dead.

US climber Seaborn Weathers of Dallas, Texas, was near the summit when the storm began. He struggled down the mountain for three days before being airlifted out from 20,000 ft. He was suffering from severe windburn and frostbite.

Less fortunate was New Zealand climber Rob Hall. During Saturday night, trapped at 25,000 ft with no tent or sleeping bag, Hall made a last radio call to his pregnant wife. He is presumed to have died.

LOS ANGELES, TUESDAY 14
Magic Johnson departs again

For the third time in his playing career Magic Johnson has retired. But this time it looks like it is for keeps.

Only four months ago Johnson, age 36, returned to the NBA. The comeback never quite lived up to the hype, and the LA Lakers' early exit from the NBA playoffs disappointed Johnson. Yet his departure surprised everyone. In a written statement he said:"It's time to move on. I am going out on my own terms."

May

S	M	T	W	T	F	S
			1	2	3	4
5	6	7	8	9	10	11
12	13	14	15	16	17	18
19	20	21	22	23	24	25
26	27	28	29	30	31	

Florida, 19
Investigators looking into the Valujet crash say they have evidence of a fire or explosion on board before the crash—oxygen cylinders in the plane's cargo are implicated. (→ May 27)

Taiwan, 20
President Lee Teng-hui, first popularly elected leader of Taiwan, is inaugurated. He says that he is willing to "make a journey of peace" to Beijing.

Washington, DC, 21
The House Judiciary Committee hears evidence of arson at black churches throughout the southern US—28 cases since the start of 1995. (→ June 9)

London, 21
Prime Minister John Major says he will obstruct EU business until the ban on exports of British beef is lifted. (→ June 21)

Jordan, MT, 22
An attempt by Colorado state senator Charles Duke to mediate a settlement with the antigovernment Freemen fails. The Freemen fly the US flag upside down in defiance. (→ June 14)

Washington, DC, 22
Bob Dole declares he would introduce tough new welfare cuts, including drug tests for recipients and no payments for unmarried teenage mothers.

Washington, DC, 22
A study reveals that there may be as many as 250,000 hacker attacks on Pentagon computer systems each year.

New Orleans, 23
A Federal Appeals Court rejects a class-action liability suit against the tobacco companies—a major victory for the tobacco industry in its effort to avoid claims worth billions of dollars.

South Korea, 23
A North Korean air-force pilot, 30-year-old Lee Chul Soo, defects to South Korea in a MiG-19 jet fighter.

Deaths

May 20. Roxanne Jones, the first black woman elected to a state Senate, at age 68, in Philadelphia.

May 21. Actor John Beradino, who appeared for 33 years as Dr. Steve Hardy on *General Hospital*, in Los Angeles, at age 79.

Washington, DC, Mon. 20
Clinton imitates GOP on welfare

President Clinton today backed a Republican governor's state welfare-reform plan, saying that if Congress passed a similar program, he would sign it right away. Speaking in his weekly radio address, the president described the reform program in Wisconsin as solid and bold, offering "hope that we can break the vicious cycle of welfare dependency."

Republicans, who have had two of their welfare-reform bills vetoed by the president, described the endorsement as a "cynical deception."

San Francisco, Thursday 23
China implicated in gunrunning

Federal agents in San Francisco have seized 2,000 AK-47 assault rifles allegedly smuggled into the US from China. Seven people have been arrested. There are indications that Chinese state-owned arms companies may have been aware of the existence of the smuggling operation.

Earlier this week, President Clinton called for the renewal of China's Most Favored Nation trade privileges, despite differences with China over human rights and copyright piracy. Some Congressmen are already suggesting that the arms-smuggling affair could again throw US-Chinese trade relations into question.

Algeria, Friday 24
Killing of monks shocks France

Islamic extremists belonging to the Armed Islamic Group (GIA) have murdered seven French Trappist monks in Algeria. The monks were kidnapped two months ago in an attempt to force France to release Islamic terrorists held in its prisons. More than 100 foreigners have been killed in Algeria since 1993.

Islamic fundamentalists are trying to overthrow the Algerian government through a terror campaign. They regard France as the government's main backer.

Washington, DC, Monday 20
Supreme Court decision is boost for gay rights

By a 6-3 majority, the Supreme Court today struck down a Colorado state constitutional amendment designed to outlaw pro-gay rights legislation. The decision was hailed by gay rights campaigners as a major victory.

The Colorado amendment banned all laws giving special protection to homosexuals. The Supreme Court ruled that it was constitutionally unfair to shut the door on any group seeking protection of its rights.

"Amendment 2 classifies homosexuals . . . to make them unequal to everyone else," Justice Anthony wrote for the court. "A state cannot so deem a class of persons a stranger to its laws."

The judgment has enraged groups fighting the spread of gay rights. A spokesman for Colorado for Family Values said the government was backing those "bent on forcing a deviant lifestyle down the throats of the American people."

Chicago, Monday 20. Michael Jordan won the NBA's Most Valuable Player award today for the fourth time, capping a brilliant return season with the Chicago Bulls. Jordan is asking for $18 million a year to remain with the Bulls for the next two years. (→ July 11)

PALERMO, TUESDAY 21

Italian police strike another blow against the Mafia

Giovanni Brusca, allegedly one of the top Mafia bosses in Sicily, was under arrest today, after 400 police surrounded the villa where he was hiding out. Brusca is thought to have been directly responsible for one of the Mafia's most notorious crimes, the assassination of popular anti-Mafia judge Giovanni Falcone in 1992.

Brusca's arrest is the latest in a series of successes for the Italian police that have put many leading Mafiosi behind bars. It is also a boost for the new Italian government of Prime Minister Romano Prodi, which has promised to crack down on organized crime.

A former Christian Democrat prime minister, Giulio Andreotti, is on trial for allegedly protecting the Mafia. The Mafiosi no longer have enough friends in high places to save them from imprisonment.

Giovanni Brusca, right, after his arrest.

WASHINGTON, DC, TUESDAY 21

500-year-old Inca ice maiden goes on display in Washington

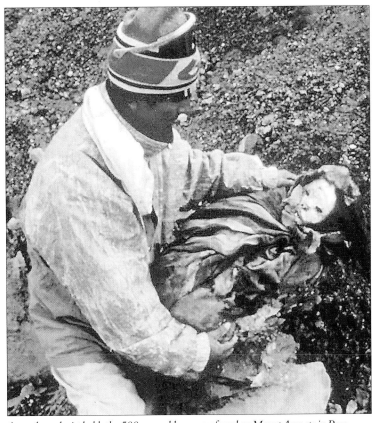

An anthropologist holds the 500-year-old mummy found on Mount Ampato in Peru.

A pubescent Inca girl sacrificed to the gods some 500 years ago went on display in Washington, DC, today. Known as "Juanita," the girl was found in a tomb on the summit of Mount Ampato in the Andes last September. Her body had been naturally mummified by the freezing conditions on the volcanic peak.

Experts have established that the girl died from a blow to the head with a club, which left no external traces. She was buried in ceremonial clothes, surrounded with offerings to the gods.

NEW YORK, MONDAY 20

Iraq accepts oil-for-food deal

President Saddam Hussein of Iraq has accepted a deal that brings the first easing of sanctions on Iraq since the 1991 Gulf War. Iraq has agreed to UN Resolution 986, drawn up last year, which allows Iraq to recommence oil exports to pay for the import of humanitarian supplies.

While Saddam Hussein and his entourage have continued to live in luxury, the Iraqi people have borne the full weight of UN-imposed economic sanctions over the last five years. Many have suffered from malnutrition and lack of basic medical supplies. The UN Secretary General Boutros Boutros Ghali said: "This resolution is based on one of the most important objectives of the United Nations, which is to alleviate the problem of poverty—and the poorest of the poor were suffering in Iraq."

Under resolution 986, Iraq will be allowed to sell $2 billion worth of oil over a six-month period. The revenue from these exports must be used to buy food and medicine, to be distributed on a fair basis among the Iraqi people. General sanctions will remain until Iraq fulfills other UN demands, including destroying all its weapons of mass destruction.

Iraq's reentry into the world oil market is expected to push oil prices lower. This could benefit President Clinton politically by halting this year's unpopular rise in gas prices in the US. (→ September 3)

LAKE VICTORIA, TUESDAY 21

Hundreds drowned in ferry disaster

More than 500 people are feared to have died when a ferry capsized on Lake Victoria today, 30 miles north of Mwanza, Tanzania. Many were teenagers returning to their homes at the end of the school term. Only 40 survivors were pulled out of the water alive. The disaster apparently occurred when the ship struck a rock.

The ferry, the Tanzanian-owned Bukoba, was officially authorized to carry 433 passengers, but eyewitnesses said many more were on board when the accident happened.

Cannes, Monday 20. Mike Leigh's *Secrets and Lies* won the Palme d'Or for best picture, and the best actress award for Brenda Blethyn (shown to the right of Leigh, above right) at the Cannes Film Festival. Canadian director David Cronenberg (above, left) won a special prize for "audacity and daring" for his film *Crash*.

S	M	T	W	T	F	S
			1	2	3	4
5	6	7	8	9	10	11
12	13	14	15	16	17	18
19	20	21	22	23	24	25
26	27	28	29	30	31	

Burma, 26
Despite intimidation and hundreds of arrests, the Burmese opposition, led by Daw Aung San Suu Kyi, hold a mass meeting in Rangoon.

Albania, 26
An election victory for the ruling conservatives in Albania leads to calls from the opposition for a campaign of protest against voting irregularities.

Florida, 27
The Valujet flight recorder, retrieved from the Everglades swamp on Sunday, confirms there was a fire on board before the crash. (→ June 18)

Orlando, 27
Chicago Bulls defeat Orlando Magic 4–0 to reach the NBA finals. Michael Jordan scores 45 points in the last game. (→ June 2)

Washington, DC, 27
In an interview with *Time* magazine Hillary Clinton reveals that she and her husband are hoping to have another child, or perhaps to adopt.

New York, 29
Ramzi Ahmed Yousef stands trial in Manhattan for allegedly planning to blow up 12 US airliners simultaneously. (→ September 5)

Los Angeles, 29
Actor Keanu Reeves leaves hospital after corrective surgery on an ankle injury that he sustained in a motorcycle accident.

Arkansas, 30
Lieutenant Governor of Arkansas Mike Huckabee stands in as governor for Jim Guy Tucker, found guilty this week in the Whitewater trial. (→ July 15)

London, 30
The marriage of the Duke and Duchess of York is officially ended. (→ June 5)

Pennsylvania, 31
Millionaire John du Pont, on trial for the murder of Olympic wrestler John Schultz, claims to be the Dalai Lama. (→ September 24)

Northern Ireland, 31
The election to all-party talks in Northern Ireland shows the strength of Sinn Fein, with 15 percent of the vote. (→ June 6)

LITTLE ROCK, TUESDAY 28

Whitewater verdict blow for Clinton

James McDougal, one of the three defendants found guilty in the Whitewater trial.

President Bill Clinton is standing high in the opinion polls, but the result of a trial in a District Court in Little Rock, Arkansas, could jeopardise his political future.

Two former business associates of Bill and Hillary Clinton, James and Susan McDougal, together with Clinton's successor as governor of Arkansas, Jim Guy Tucker, were today found guilty on a range of counts connected with illegal loans. All are appealing the verdicts.

The White House was swift to point out that "the president had nothing to do with the allegations that were the subject of the trial." But he gave videotaped evidence for the defense, and his credibility is called into question by the verdicts.

Independent counsel Kenneth W. Starr and a senate committee are investigating the Whitewater land development, in which the Clintons and McDougals were partners. These investigations are sure to proceed with renewed energy. (→ August 20)

MOSCOW, MONDAY 27

Yeltsin announces accord with Chechens

After 17 months' fighting that has cost over 30,000 lives, the war in Chechnya may be over. Russian president Boris Yeltsin and Chechen rebel leader Zelimkhan Yandarbiyev agreed today in the Kremlin to halt hostilities at the start of next month. The Chechen rebels, some wearing battle dress, were flown into Moscow only two hours before the agreement was announced. They calculated that the Russians would keep a promise of safe conduct back to Chechnya.

The two sides made no effort to agree on the fundamental issues that divide them. The Chechen rebels are still demanding independence, while the Russians regard Chechnya as part of their national territory. But both sides need a cease-fire. The rebels have recently suffered military setbacks, while Yeltsin cannot win the presidential election next month without peace in Chechnya. (→ June 10)

Boris Yeltsin (left) meeting with Chechen rebel leader Zelimkhan Yandarbiyev (in combat fatigues, right) at the Kremlin.

BEVERLY HILLS, FRIDAY 31
Guru of LSD drops out for ever

Timothy Leary, the prophet of the 1960s psychedelic revolution, has died at age 75. Leary was a Harvard psychologist before he discovered LSD and advised a generation to "tune in, turn on, drop out." The vicissitudes of his career took him to prison and to a spell as a fugitive. In his later years he became a proponent of the liberating effects of electronic communication. He posted updates on his losing battle with prostate cancer on the World Wide Web.

Psychedelic guru Timothy Leary.

JERUSALEM, FRIDAY 31
Israeli election puts peace process in doubt

It was a narrow victory, but a decisive one: Benjamin Netanyahu is the new Israeli prime minister, winning by 30,000 votes. He polled 1,501,023 votes as against 1,471,566 for the incumbent, Shimon Peres.

Netanyahu pledged to continue the peace process. But discontent over security was a major cause for the swing against Peres's Labor Party. Netanyahu's Likud alliance campaigned on a platform of getting tough with the Arabs.

Ahmed Korei, a Palestinian leader, warned: "The region will return to tension and violence, maybe wars, if the new Israeli team implements its election slogans." (→ July 9)

New Israeli prime minister Benjamin Netanyahu (right) during his election campaign.

Denver, Wednesday 29. Colorado Avalanche qualify for the NHL finals against the Florida Panthers after knocking out the Detroit Red Wings tonight, 4-1. Right-winger Claude Lemieux (above) was ejected from the game in the first period. (→ June 10)

NEW DELHI, TUESDAY 28
India changes leadership again

India's leader H.D. Deve Gowda.

Only thirteen days ago, Hindu nationalists hailed their leader, Atal Bihari Vajpayee, as Indian prime minister. But today he is out of office following his party's inability to assemble a majority, and it is the turn of the little-known H.D. Deve Gowda to govern the world's most populous democracy. He heads a coalition of left-wing and regional parties. (→ June 12)

INDIANAPOLIS, SUNDAY 26
Indy car split fails to dampen racing drama

The Indianapolis 500 had a rival this year—the US 500, raced in Michigan on the same day. The two-race scenario resulted from a split between the Indy Racing League and the Championship Auto Racing Team (CART), representing many of the top names in the sport.

CART thought its star-studded US 500 was sure to scoop the headlines, but in the event it lost out on drama. The Michigan race turned out a predictable win for championship leader Jimmy Vasser. In Indianapolis, a relative unknown, Buddy Lazier, won by the narrowest of margins—after arriving at the race on crutches. Two months ago Lazier suffered severe back injuries in an accident. He needed a special cockpit to drive.

S	M	T	W	T	F	S
						1
2	3	4	5	6	7	8
9	10	11	12	13	14	15
16	17	18	19	20	21	22
23	24	25	26	27	28	29
30						

Southern Pines, NC, 2
Defending golf champion, Annika Sorenstam, 25, from Stockholm wins the US Women's Open by six strokes.

Washington, DC, 2
A team of scientists at the National Oceanic and Atmospheric Administration announces that levels of ozone-depleting chemicals in the air are declining.

Seattle, 2
The Seattle SuperSonics beat the Utah Jazz 90–86 to join the Chicago Bulls in the NBA finals. (→ June 16)

New York, 2
At the 50th Tony Awards, the musicals *Rent* and *Bring in 'da Noise, Bring in 'da Funk* each garner four awards.

St. Petersburg, 3
Leading Russian reformer and Yeltsin supporter, Anatoly Sobchak, is voted out of office as mayor of St. Petersburg.

London, 3
Microwaves transmitted by mobile phones may cause asthma, cancer, and other diseases, according to evidence assembled for a BBC TV program.

Ukraine, 3
President Leonid Kuchman announces the completion of the removal of the last nuclear warheads from the Ukraine.

Princeton, NJ, 5
President Clinton proposes a $1,500 per student tax credit for the first two years of college to help make higher education as universal as high school.

New York, 5
The Duchess of York sells her autobiography to Simon & Schuster for $1.3 million despite signing a confidentiality clause as part of her divorce settlement.

Panama City, 6
The Helms-Burton Law tightening the US blockade of Cuba is condemned by all but the US at the annual OAS summit.

Philadelphia, 6
After positive comments about Hitler made by Cincinnati Reds owner Marge Schott on ESPN last month, the executive council instructs her to relinquish control of her team or else face suspension.

VIRGINIA, SATURDAY 1
Brutal murders in national park

Two female hikers have been brutally killed in Shenandoah National Park, Virginia. Park rangers found the bodies of Julianne Williams of St. Cloud, Minnesota, and Lollie Winans of Unity, Maine, near the Appalachian Trail. The young women, both in their twenties, had last been seen alive on May 24.

The deaths have raised concerns about safety in national parks, visited by 270 million people a year. Federal officials counter that only 13 homicides occurred in national parks last year.

London, Saturday 8. The biggest soccer tournament held in England for 30 years—Euro '96—opened today at Wembley stadium in a blaze of pageantry. The colorful opening ceremony included a mock-medieval representation of the slaying of the dragon by St. George.

BELFAST, THURSDAY 6
Mitchell appointment causes row

Senator George Mitchell, President Clinton's envoy, is to chair the all-party talks on the future of Northern Ireland that open next week. The appointment was greeted with outrage by Ulster Unionists and by some British Conservative politicians. They believe Senator Mitchell is sympathetic to the Irish nationalists.

One Conservative member of the British parliament, Terry Dicks, has threatened to withdraw support from John Major's government over the issue. The Conservative party has a majority of only one in the House of Commons. (→ June 10)

CHICAGO, WEDNESDAY 5
Di takes on basketball and wins

As part of a US tour to raise $1.5 million for breast cancer research, Princess Diana was in Chicago today, visiting hospitals and starring at a fund-raising dinner. The dinner coincided with the Chicago Bulls' opening game in the NBA playoffs.

But Princess Di proved a greater pull, with people paying up to $4,500 for a seat. Even Michael Jordan's mother, Deloris, attended. Illinois Governor Jim Edgar said the princess was "the only person I know who can push Michael Jordan from the front page."

Enthusiastic fans greet Princess Diana outside Cook County Hospital in Chicago.

FRENCH GUIANA, TUESDAY 4
Ariane 5 launch ends in disaster

The European space shuttle launcher seconds before it is exploded.

Scientists and officials of the European Space Agency were in a state of shock tonight after the Ariane 5 rocket had to be blown up on its maiden launch. The rocket's payload—four Cluster satellites—was also lost in the disaster.

Ground controllers activated the explosion 66 seconds after liftoff because the rocket had veered off course and was beginning to break up. Neither the rocket nor its payload was insured. The value of the satellites alone is estimated at $750 million.

François Fillon, French space minister, said a second Ariane 5 launch would go ahead. "We knew the risks we ran," he added.

Alaska swept by worst fire in its history

Firefighters are unable to save another home as the fire continues to spread. Experts believe the fire may have been started by fireworks.

It is proving to be one of the worst years in living memory for wildfires in many parts of the western US and Alaska. In the most recent example a wildfire has forced more than a thousand people to flee their homes and ravaged more than 40,000 acres of Alaskan wilderness north of the state capital, Anchorage. The fire started last weekend. Over 1,000 firefighters have been tackling the blaze but it remains untamed.

The fire has forced the evacuation of the settlements of Houston and Big Lake, as well as a state prison farm and hundreds of wilderness homes. The only highway running between Anchorage and Fairbanks has been closed intermittently.

High winds have driven the fire south toward Anchorage, which has a population of 225,000. The curtain of smoke is clearly visible from the city, but the main urban area is protected by a narrow bay.

FBI revelations put Hillary Clinton on the defensive

The Senate Whitewater committee revealed today that Hillary Clinton's fingerprints have been found on her legal billing records, lost for two years and discovered in the White House in January. The fingerprints of five other people, including Clinton aides, were also found on the documents.

The FBI was ordered to carry out a fingerprint analysis of the controversial billing documents by Whitewater special prosecutor Kenneth Starr. The results of the tests are open to conflicting interpretations.

Republicans are sure to insist that the presence of Hillary Clinton's fingerprints shows she had some part in concealing the billing records, which some believe were spirited away from the office of White House counsel Vincent Foster after his suicide in July 1993. But the White House claims Hillary Clinton never denied she at some time handled the documents. The FBI cannot date the fingerprints. (→ June 18)

Pol Pot reported dead

Pol Pot, leader of the Khmer Rouge.

According to reports circulating in southeast Asia, Khmer Rouge leader Pol Pot, one of this century's most notorious political figures, may be dead or dying of malaria. Pol Pot ruled Cambodia from 1975 to 1979, directing a reign of terror that may have caused the deaths of one million people. The Khmer Rouge is now fighting a vicious guerrilla war against the Cambodian government.

Los Angeles, Saturday 1. Tom Cruise's *Mission: Impossible* is showing on more than 4,000 screens in the US. Director Brian De Palma said, "Tom always wanted to make it the smartest movie possible."

Gingrich targets Mayor Barry

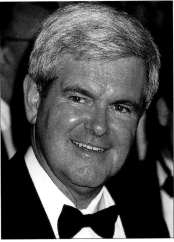

House speaker Newt Gingrich.

Newt Gingrich has today called on Washington mayor Marion Barry to make a public apology for comparing the city's financial control board to the Nazis. Gingrich warned that unless Barry cooperated with the control board, home rule would be revoked and a Congress appointee would run the district.

June

Texas, 9
Two black churches are torched in Greenville, Texas, and the KKK initials are painted in the town. (→ June 12)

Paris, 9
Yevgeny Kafelnikov becomes the first Russian to win a major tennis title after he beats Michael Stich in five sets in the final of the French Open.

Northern Ireland, 10
Historic all-party talks on the future of Northern Ireland begin at Stormont, east Belfast, but without Sinn Fein, excluded because of continuing IRA terrorism. (→ June 15)

Miami, 10
Colorado Avalanche beats the Florida Panthers 1–0 to take the ice hockey Stanley Cup. Joe Sakic is named the Most Valuable Player.

Southern Lebanon, 10
Five Israeli soldiers are killed and eight are wounded in an ambush in southern Lebanon by Hizbollah guerrillas.

Russia, 10
Russian and Chechen negotiators sign a deal promising the withdrawal of all Russian troops from Chechnya by the end of August. (→ August 16)

New York, 11
British Airways and American Airlines announce an alliance to create the world's largest air network.

Dallas, 11
Thirteen-year-old LeAnn Rimes tops the country music charts with her song *Blue*.

Washington, DC, 12
Republican Trent Lott takes over as Senate leader from Bob Dole, who bid an emotional farewell to the Senate on Tuesday.

India, 12
India's new prime minister, H. D. Deve Gowda, wins a vote of confidence in parliament and will rule as head of the United Front coalition.

New York, 14
John J. Royster admits to a series of horrific killings and attacks on women in New York, including a woman attacked in Central Park last week. He was originally arrested for failing to pay for a subway ticket.

IRA bomb blasts Manchester city center, injuring 200

The Manchester bomb site—the explosion caused millions of pounds' worth of damage.

A massive IRA bomb devastated the heart of Manchester today. About 200 people were injured, nine of them seriously, including a pregnant woman expecting her baby in eight days.

After a telephone warning was received at 9:40 a.m., police identified the location of the bomb, in a parked van. They evacuated the immediate area, but when the bomb exploded at 12:40 p.m. the size of the explosion was such that shards of glass flew up to a half mile across an area crowded with Saturday shoppers.

Prime Minister John Major called the bombing "a dreadful act," and President Clinton expressed "deep outrage." It seems set to destroy the remaining credibility of Sinn Fein leader Gerry Adams in the US.

More than 75,000 are evacuated from Manchester's city center before the explosion.

US, Monday 10. *The Rock*, a hostage-rescue thriller starring Nicholas Cage (right) and Sean Connery overtakes *Mission: Impossible* as the top US box-office draw. The film was shot on location on Alcatraz despite setbacks such as no electricity and crumbling foundations.

Largest-ever financial fraud revealed

Japan's Sumitomo Corporation has announced losses of around $2.5 billion in ten years' unauthorized dealing by its one-time head copper trader, Yasuo Hamanaka. The fraud is believed to be the biggest ever recorded, far exceeding the estimated $1.2 billion losses caused by British trader Nick Leeson at Barings Bank.

Mr. Hamanaka, known as "the 5 percent man" because he was believed to control that proportion of the world copper market, falsified books and records to conceal his activities. His actions were uncovered by regulators in the US and Britain.

FBI director condemns the White House

The FBI director, Louis J. Freeh, has delivered a stinging rebuke to the White House for "egregious violations of privacy." The condemnation came after an inquiry revealed that White House staff had improperly requested FBI files on 408 people, some of them key Republicans.

"Filegate," as it has been called, is another blow to President Clinton's credibility. The president has apologized for what he claims was a bureaucratic error. (→ June 26)

Bangkok, Sunday 9. Thailand's King Bhumibol, age 68, the world's longest-serving monarch, today celebrated 50 years on the throne with traditional pomp. As part of the Jubilee celebrations, 26,000 prisoners will be released from Thailand's jails.

Freemen surrender after long siege

After a siege lasting 81 days, the last 16 members of the antigovernment Freemen group have surrendered to federal agents without a struggle. The Freemen had declared that federal law did not apply to Justus Township, their ranch near Jordan, Montana. FBI Director Louis J. Freeh claimed the outcome vindicated the strategy of "honest and persistent attempts at negotiation."

Clinton denounces church burnings

President Clinton prays during a visit to the rebuilt Mount Zion church in South Carolina.

President Bill Clinton today called on Americans of all races to unite in rebuilding black churches destroyed by arson and resisting the divisive effects of racism. He was visiting one of more than 30 churches burned down across the southern US in the last 18 months. Standing in the car park of the new Mount Zion church in Greeleyville, South Carolina, not far from the charred remains of the old church up the road, President Clinton said: "I want to ask every citizen, as we stand on this hallowed ground together, to help rebuild our churches, to restore hope, to show the forces of hatred they cannot win."

The church-burning issue came to the forefront of national politics last weekend, when southern church ministers lobbied Washington, DC, and President Clinton made the church burnings the theme of his weekly radio address.

There is as yet no evidence of a conspiracy to link the arsons, nor are all of them believed to be necessarily an expression of racism. Few of the cases have been solved.

Not everyone was convinced by the president's call for healing and reconciliation. The Reverend Jesse Jackson, who spoke in Greeleyville before the president's arrival, denounced right-wing Republicans for encouraging a climate of racism. Jackson was supported by other black speakers.

The president refused to endorse this approach, saying that the issue of church burnings must be "kept out of politics." (→ June 20)

Jazz world mourns the loss of singer Ella Fitzgerald

Jazz legend Ella Fitzgerald: A shy, self-effacing figure who set new standards for singing.

Ella Fitzgerald, jazz's "first lady of song," has died, at age 79, at her home in Beverly Hills, California. In her later years she had suffered severe health problems connected with chronic diabetes. Tragically, in 1993 both her legs had to be amputated below the knees.

Ella Fitzgerald's singing encompassed a variety of styles, but she is perhaps most famous for perfecting the technique of wordless vocal improvisation known as scat. In a career that spanned 60 years, she recorded with some of the greatest names in jazz, including Louis Armstrong, Duke Ellington, and Count Basie.

Songwriter Ira Gershwin once said: "I never knew how good our songs were until I heard Ella Fitzgerald sing them." Today famous vocalists rushed to pay tribute to her memory. Singer Tony Bennett said: "She was the lady who taught us all how to sing. She was the spirit."

S	M	T	W	T	F	S
						1
2	3	4	5	6	7	8
9	10	11	12	13	14	15
16	17	18	19	20	21	22
23	24	25	26	27	28	29
30						

Detroit, 16
US golfer Steve Jones, a rank outsider, wins the US Open Championship at the Oakland Hills course.

Beijing, 17
The Chinese government agrees to crack down on copyright piracy to avert a trade war with the US.

Sacramento, CA, 18
Theodore Kaczynski, held on a charge of bomb-making since April 3, is formally charged with carrying out bomb attacks attributed to the so-called Unabomber.

Washington, DC, 18
Valujet, the low-fare airline at the focus of concerns over airplane safety standards ever since the Everglades air crash in May, has voluntarily halted operations as the investigations continue. (→ September 26)

San Jose, CA, 19
Richard A. Davis is found guilty of the "slumber-party" killing of 12-year-old Polly Klaas in 1993.(→ September 26)

Little Rock, 19
Lawyers reveal that Whitewater special prosecutor Kenneth Starr is to name Bruce Lindsey, one of President Clinton's closest advisers, as an unindicted co-conspirator in the trial of two Arkansas bankers. (→ July 8)

Cleveland, 19
Albert Belle, baseball's major league home-run leader this season, has a five-match suspension reduced to three matches on appeal.

San Francisco, 20
The California Supreme Court rules that the "three strikes" law imposing life prison terms for persistent offenders is not mandatory. Judges may overrule it if they think that the sentence would be too harsh.

Washington, DC, 20
President Clinton meets with governors of southern states to discuss a response to arson attacks on black churches.

Florence, Italy, 21
At a summit of European leaders, British prime minister John Major calls off his campaign of obstruction of EU business in return for the promise of a staged lifting of the ban on British beef exports.

WASHINGTON, DC, TUESDAY 18

Report accuses Hillary Clinton of cover-up

In an 800-page report released today, the Republican majority on the Senate Whitewater Committee has accused Hillary Clinton of a "pattern of abuses," but has stopped short of any specific allegations of lawbreaking.

The Republicans claim that Hillary Clinton was involved in all the areas they investigated, from fraudulent land deals in Arkansas to the alleged concealment of her legal billing records. Senator Alfonse D'Amato, chairing the committee, said the Clinton presidency had "misused its power, circumvented the limits on its authority, and attempted to manipulate the truth."

The committee's Democrat minority strongly dissented from its critical conclusions. Their report asserts: "The American people deserve to know and now can take comfort in knowing that this yearlong investigation shows no misconduct or abuse of power by their president or first lady." (→ June 19)

CHICAGO, SUNDAY 16

The Chicago Bulls crush the Seattle SuperSonics to grab the NBA title

The streets of Chicago are heaving with supporters of the victorious Chicago Bulls.

Celebrating basketball fans took to the streets tonight as the Chicago Bulls clinched their fourth NBA Championship in six seasons. The Seattle SuperSonics put up a good enough show to take the best-of-seven series to the sixth game, but in the end they were rolled over by the combination of Dennis Rodman, Scottie Pippen, and Michael Jordan, voted most valuable player in the finals.

Near tears, Michael Jordan dedicated the victory to his murdered father. "This is for Daddy," he said.

New Zealand, Monday 17. Mount Ruapehu volcano, situated in the heart of North Island—180 miles north of the capital, Wellington—has erupted, spewing out rocks and ash. The nearby town of Turangi, where residents have been advised to stay indoors, is covered with a layer of ash, and airports within 100 miles of the 9,000-ft high mountain have been closed.

Russia's elections too close to call

A former army officer holds the future of Russia in his hands after the closely contested first round of presidential elections last weekend. General Alexander Lebed polled under 15 percent of the vote, but with the two main contenders—current president Boris Yeltsin and the communist challenger Gennadi Zyuganov—evenly poised for the second-round run-off on July 3, Lebed's supporters hold the balance.

Yeltsin headed the first-round poll with 35 percent of the vote, narrowly ahead of Zyuganov with 32 percent. Ultranationalist Vladimir Zhirinovsky, once favored to succeed Yeltsin, polled only 6 percent, a percentage point less than the reformer Grigori Yavlinsky. Former president Mikhail Gorbachev won an ignominious 0.5 percent of votes cast.

Topping the poll was a remarkable comeback for Yeltsin, who looked unelectable only a few months ago. The energy of his performance in the campaign astonished observers who had doubted his health would survive the pressure of electioneering.

Yeltsin's supporters made full use of their control over the media and lavish financial backing. The communists were virtually barred from television during the campaign and were short of funds. (→ June 20)

Current president, Boris Yeltsin, finds new vigor as he hits the campaign trail.

Challenger, communist Gennadi Zyuganov, with supporters at a welcoming ceremony.

Yeltsin purges hardliners

As political maneuvering continues in the wake of Sunday's first round of Russian elections, President Boris Yeltsin today announced the dismissal of the three leading hardliners in his regime, security chiefs General Alexander Korzhakov and General Mikhail Barsukov, and First Deputy Prime Minister Oleg Soskovets.

General Korzhakov was regarded as Yeltsin's closest aide and the second most powerful man in Russia. He was notoriously ruthless in his use of surveillance and police powers.

The dismissals follow the sacking of Defense Minister General Pavel Grachev on Tuesday, and the appointment of General Alexander Lebed as secretary of the security council. The elections had left Lebed as Russia's power broker, choosing between Yeltsin and communist Gennadi Zyuganov as next Russian president. Lebed had made it clear that he favored Yeltsin over the communist candidate. "We have gone past communism," the general said, "and have left this shore for ever."

Lebed was in a strong enough position to demand large concessions from the president in return for his support. Whether these concessions included the dismissal of Korzhakov is not yet known. (→ July 4)

US Olympic trials get underway in Atlanta

Carl Lewis qualifies for the long jump at the US Olympic selection trials.

At the track and field trials currently being held at Atlanta, two veteran US athletes have shown they still have that special Olympic quality. On Tuesday Mary Slaney, now 37, a top-flight runner since the age of 14, powered into a qualifying place in the 5000 meters. Carl Lewis, 34, one of the greatest names in athletics history, qualified for the Olympic long jump by a margin of 1 in. He is the first US track and field athlete to qualify for five consecutive Olympic Games.

The athlete tipped for the most eye-catching performances in the Games is sprinter Michael Johnson. Already qualified for the 400 meters, he intends to attempt the 200 meters as well, an Olympic double never yet achieved. (→ June 23)

England, Tuesday 18. The first day of Royal Ascot brought the traditional array of spectacular millinery. Designer Isabell Kristensen, pictured above, wore one of her own creations.

June

Atlanta, 23
US sprinter Michael Johnson breaks the world's oldest record in a championship event, the men's 200 meters, in trials for the Olympic Games.

Cairo, 23
An emergency Arab summit calls on Israel to continue withdrawing from occupied territory or endanger the peace process. The Israeli government rejects the communiqué.

Washington, DC, 24
The Supreme Court agrees to delay President Clinton's sexual harassment case, brought by Paula Jones, until after the presidential elections.

Washington, DC, 26
"Filegate" hearings investigating the White House acquisition of hundreds of FBI files on Republicans begin.

Venice, 26
Experts investigating the Fenice opera house fire of five months ago conclude that it was started deliberately.

Kabul, Afghanistan, 26
As the former rebel leader Gulbuddin Hekmatyar is sworn in as new prime minister of Afghanistan, guerrillas assault Kabul with rockets, killing 64.

The Hague, Netherlands, 27
The Bosnian War Crimes Tribunal begins hearing the cases of Serb leaders Radovan Karadzic and Ratko Mladic, both accused of genocide. (→ July 11)

Wimbledon, 28
Seeded players crash in the first week of Wimbledon: Andre Agassi, Michael Chang, Jim Courier, and Monica Seles are all defeated; and Boris Becker pulls out with a wrist injury. (→ July 6)

Lyons, France, 28
The Group of Seven top industrialized nations, at their summit in Lyons, agree to unite in the fight against organized crime and terrorism.

Lexington, VA, 28
The Supreme Court rules that the all-male Virginia Military Institute must admit women or lose state funding.

Deaths
June 27. Albert R. "Cubby" Broccoli, film producer best known for his 17 Bond films, in Beverly Hills, at age 87.

BANGLADESH, MONDAY 24
New leader promises reforms

Sheikha Hasina Wajed, the new prime minister of Bangladesh who was sworn in on Sunday, has vowed sweeping democratic reforms. One of the world's poorest nations, Bangladesh has had military rule for most of its 25-year existence. This year's free elections only occurred after waves of popular protest. Sheikha Hasina is the daughter of Sheikh Mujibur Rahman, who led Bangladesh to independence in 1971.

Sheikha Hasina Wajed.

WASHINGTON, DC, SATURDAY 29
Clinton angered by salacious rumor

Former FBI official Gary Aldrich, after defending his book on ABC television.

The press is having a field day with the juiciest Clinton rumor yet— that the president frequently slips out of the White House for trysts in Washington's Marriott Hotel with an unnamed female. The undocumented allegation, which appeared in *Unlimited Access*, a book by former FBI official Gary Aldrich, was angrily dismissed by a White House spokesman as "a fabrication." A Marriott Hotel official, Kirby Smith, said: "The claims are to the best of our knowledge inaccurate." (→ July 3)

ATHENS, WEDNESDAY 26
Thousands mourn a hero of Greece

Pallbearers carrying Papandreou's coffin during the pomp-filled procession through Athens.

The streets of Athens were lined with weeping crowds today as the body of Andreas Papandreou, Greece's most charismatic political leader, was carried to its last resting place. Socialist prime minister until last January, Papandreou was a prominent figure in Greek political life for 30 years. He survived crises ranging from imprisonment after a coup in 1967 to a trial for corruption in 1991. His womanizing was legendary: seven years ago, at the age of 70, he married a flight attendant 36 years his junior.

CAPE TOWN, SUNDAY 23
Archbishop Tutu bows out gracefully

Desmond Tutu today led a farewell service at St. George's cathedral, Cape Town, before his retirement as Anglican Archbishop. During the harsh years of apartheid, he used his ecclesiastical authority to oppose white rule and encourage South Africa on the road to democracy.

Archbishop Desmond Tutu.

No seances at the White House

Journalist Bob Woodward's new book *The Choice* has implied that Hillary Clinton had conversations with dead heroines such as Eleanor Roosevelt. But the notion of spiritualism at the White House was swiftly quashed. Jean Houston, the adviser who led the sessions to which Woodward referred, described them as a creative exercise, "a role-playing technique used in every corporation in the world." She said she was not a psychic and did not believe in spirits.

Paris, Tuesday 25. TV reporter Christiane Amanpour becomes the world's highest paid foreign correspondent after signing a deal with both CNN and CBS for $2 million a year.

DUBLIN, WEDNESDAY 26

Crime journalist murdered

Veronica Guerin, a journalist who specialized in exposés of Ireland's criminal underworld, was shot dead in Dublin today. A motorbike pulled up alongside her car at traffic lights and the pillion passenger opened fire with a handgun. Police believe it was a contract killing.

Ms. Guerin, who was married with a seven-year-old child, had pursued her investigations of Dublin gang bosses in the face of extreme intimidation. In 1994 she was shot in the leg by an intruder in her home. "I just would not give in to them," she said.

Truck bomb kills 19 US servicemen

US airmen remember their 19 comrades killed in the bomb attack at an emotional memorial service held in Dhahran on Friday.

The bomb-blasted apartment building where US and other foreign servicemen were housed.

Nineteen US airmen have been killed in a truck bomb attack on an apartment building in Saudi Arabia. The men were among the 2,900 US servicemen stationed at the King Abdul Aziz Air Base near Dhahran.

The 3,000 lb bomb was left in a parking lot just outside the perimeter fence of the US military compound. It devastated the men's quarters, which also housed British and French military personnel. As well as killing 19, the blast injured more than 160 people.

Although no group has yet admitted responsibility for the bomb attack, it is believed to be the work of Saudi militants hostile to the US presence in their country and to the rule of the Saudi royal family. The attack may be a direct response to the execution of four Saudis on May 31.

The US has flown in 40 FBI antiterrorist specialists to investigate the attack. Promising to punish the terrorists responsible for the bombing, President Clinton said: "Anyone who attacks one American attacks every American, and we protect and defend our own." (→ September 16)

S	M	T	W	T	F	S
	1	2	3	4	5	6
7	8	9	10	11	12	13
14	15	16	17	18	19	20
21	22	23	24	25	26	27
28	29	30	31			

Northern Territory, Australia, 1
The world's first law permitting voluntary euthanasia comes into force here today. It is being contested in the courts. (→ September 25)

Ulan Bator, Mongolia, 1
The Democratic Union wins a landslide in Mongolian elections, ending 75 years of control by the communists.

New York, 3
Newsweek magazine reports that recent allegations that President Clinton slips out of the White House regularly for romantic meetings with a woman are based purely on a rumor passed on by a conservative journalist.

Los Angeles, 3
Investigators are looking for an explanation for the power outage that blacked out 15 western states—high summer temperatures may have caused a circuit breaker on a key power grid to shut down through overloading.

Chicago, 3
Charges are dropped against three men—Dennis Williams, Kenneth Adams, and Willie Rainge—who have been in jail for 18 years for murders they did not commit. Two of the men were on death row.

US, 3
Singer Garth Brooks, whose US album sales are now second only to the Beatles, breaks concert-ticket records at nearly every stop on his new tour.

St. Petersburg, FL, 3
Researchers claim they have found the cause of death of 158 manatees this year, blaming "red tide," a toxic build-up of natural organisms off the Florida coast.

Scottown, OH, 4
Eight people are killed in a blaze in a fireworks store after a customer allegedly lit a firework on a dare. Todd Hall, 24, is charged with manslaughter.

Oslo, 5
Namibian Frankie Fredericks beats US world-record holder Michael Johnson in the Bislett Games' 200-meter race.

Wimbledon, 6
Steffi Graf wins the women's singles final at Wimbledon, defeating Arantxa Sanchez Vicario 6-3, 7-5 in 88 minutes. (→ July 7)

SANTA MONICA, MONDAY 1

Actress Margaux Hemingway is found dead

Margaux Hemingway, the 41-year-old granddaughter of novelist Ernest Hemingway, was found dead today in her apartment in Santa Monica. Investigators believe she died of natural causes. Once a Hollywood star and the best-paid model in the world, Ms. Hemingway struggled in recent years with alcoholism, bulimia, and epilepsy brought on by drinking. An autopsy is scheduled for Wednesday.

Hemingway: Cause of death is unknown.

PHOENIX, MONDAY 1

Militia charged with bomb plot

Federal agents in Arizona have arrested 12 people for allegedly plotting to bomb government buildings. The twelve—ten men and two women—are said to be members of an antigovernment paramilitary group, the "Viper Militia."

US Attorney General Janet Reno said that the militia planned to bomb a number of targets, including the offices of the Bureau of Alcohol, Tobacco, and Firearms, and of the Immigration and Naturalization Service in Phoenix.

An undercover federal agent apparently infiltrated the militia group and covertly videotaped its meetings. The organization is said to have accumulated large quantities of ammonium nitrate, the main substance that was used to make the bomb that killed 169 people in Oklahoma City last year.

WIMBLEDON, SATURDAY 6

Washington makes Wimbledon final

MaliVai Washington—the first black player since Arthur Ashe to reach a Wimbledon final.

The Wimbledon tennis tournament lost many stars early this year, with crowd pullers Andre Agassi and Boris Becker out in the first week. And the British summer weather was a party-pooper, with rain stopping play time and again. But at least a new name is guaranteed for the men's champions list. The title will be contested tomorrow by two unseeded players, MaliVai Washington of the US and Dutchman Richard Krajicek. The only unseeded player to win Wimbledon before was Boris Becker in 1985. (→ July 7)

US, Tuesday 2. Sci-fi blockbuster *Independence Day* opens around the country, with some theaters scheduling 24-hour showings and critics predicting that it will be the "monster hit" of the summer.

JERUSALEM, MONDAY 1
Ex-nanny knocks Netanyahu's wife

Israel's new prime minister Benjamin Netanyahu came under attack from an unexpected direction today when his family's ex-nanny denounced his wife on Israeli army radio.

The nanny, Tanya Shaw, claimed that Israel's First Lady flew into a rage and threw her out on the street after a row about burned soup. Ms. Shaw painted a grim picture of the family's life, describing Mrs. Netanyahu as unstable and obsessed with cleanliness.

The official reason given for the nanny's dismissal was that she posed a security threat. A statement described Ms. Shaw as disturbed and prone to "outbursts of violence."

Cape Canaveral, Tuesday 2. Lockheed Martin today unveiled plans for the X-33, a $1-billion wedge-shaped rocket ship that it will develop for NASA to replace the aging space shuttle fleet by 2012.

MOSCOW, THURSDAY 4
Yeltsin wins, but fitness still in doubt

Boris Yeltsin doing the twist with a Russian pop group—his reelection campaign was filled with similar displays of youthful energy.

Boris Yeltsin has succeeded in his campaign for reelection as president of Russia. In the second round of voting, completed yesterday, Yeltsin received 53.7 percent of the vote, versus 40.4 percent for his communist opponent Gennadi Zyuganov.

The president adopted a conciliatory tone in his moment of triumph. "Let us not divide the country into victors and vanquished," he said. The loser was less moderate. Zyuganov told reporters that if economic and social conditions continued to deteriorate, he would "not rule out the possibility of mass riots."

Most observers, however, felt that Yeltsin was less threatened by the possible deterioration of the Russian economy than by the deterioration of his own health. Determined to demonstrate his fitness to rule, the president put on some startling displays of youthful energy during the long election campaign. But it is still considered doubtful whether his health will hold up through a full four-year term in office. (→ July 15)

Yeltsin seizes another dancing opportunity.

LONDON, FRIDAY 5
Diana receives Charles's terms for divorce

Princess Diana at a recent charity event.

The Prince of Wales's lawyers last night presented Princess Diana with his terms for a divorce settlement, ending a ten-week deadlock that has stalled progress toward ending their 15-year marriage.

Although the terms have not been made public, there is press speculation that the settlement will cost the Prince around $30 million. (→ July 12)

DALLAS, WEDNESDAY 3
Dallas Cowboys star goes on trial

Michael Irvin, a receiver for this year's Superbowl winners, the Dallas Cowboys, stands trial today for possession of drugs. Irvin was allegedly discovered by police in a motel room with two topless dancers, cocaine, marijuana, and drug paraphernalia.

The case took a further bizarre turn when a Dallas police officer, Johnnie Hernandez, was arrested for allegedly trying to hire a hitman to kill Irvin. Hernandez is involved with one of the two women found in Irvin's motel room.

S	M	T	W	T	F	S
	1	2	3	4	5	6
7	8	9	10	11	12	13
14	15	16	17	18	19	20
21	22	23	24	25	26	27
28	29	30	31			

Vancouver, 7
Peter Piot, UN AIDS program director, reports before the start of the eleventh International AIDS Conference that rates of infection are slowing down.

Cape Canaveral, FL, 7
The space shuttle Columbia returns to Earth after the longest-ever shuttle flight, 16 days and 22 hours.

Wimbledon, 7
Dutch tennis player Richard Krajicek wins the Wimbledon men's singles final, defeating MaliVai Washington of the US in straight sets.

Washington, DC, 8
President Clinton gives a video deposition in the case of two Arkansas bankers charged with making illegal contributions to Clinton's 1990 gubernatorial election campaign.
(→ August 1)

Washington, DC, 9
The Senate passes a bill raising the minimum wage to $4.75 an hour this year and $5.15 an hour next year.

Washington, DC, 9
Mary Schiavo resigns as the inspector-general of the Transportation Department. She was outspokenly critical of the Federal Aviation Administration in the wake of the Valujet crash in the Florida Everglades.

New York, 10
A heavyweight bout in Madison Square Gardens between Andrew Galota and Riddick Bowe ends in brawling throughout the arena after the crowd contests the referee's decision to stop the fight.

Chicago, 11
Michael Jordan agrees to stay with the Chicago Bulls for one year, for an alleged $25 million.

London, 12
The Prince and Princess of Wales agree on terms for divorce. The financial settlement is worth $22 million. (→ July 15)

Deaths
July 12. John Chancellor, NBC television journalist, in Princeton, New Jersey, at age 68.

NORTHERN IRELAND, FRIDAY 12

Violence flares on the streets of Ulster

Catholics riot in protest across the province: In Londonderry masked men and boys throw Molotov cocktails at abandoned cars and buildings.

The Northern Ireland peace process appears to be in ruins after the worst rioting in the province for many years. The trouble began on Sunday when RUC Chief Constable Sir Hugh Annesley banned Protestant Orangemen from marching through a Catholic area in Drumcree, near Portadown. As Loyalists confronted police at Drumcree, Protestants took to the streets across the province, blockading roads and driving many Catholics from their homes.

On Thursday, faced with threats of even worse violence, the RUC let the Drumcree march go ahead. The unsurprising result of this U-turn was widespread rioting by Catholics, outraged at what they saw as capitulation to the Loyalists. (→ July 14)

Police protect the Orangemen's parade.

WASHINGTON, DC, TUESDAY 9

A cool summit reaffirms Israel's ties with the US

Benjamin Netanyahu and President Clinton present a "united front" at the press conference.

President Clinton and Israel's new prime minister, Benjamin Netanyahu, met in the White House today and declared a shared commitment to peace in the Middle East. But the meeting showed none of the warmth that had characterized the president's relationship with the previous Israeli leader, Shimon Peres.

At a press conference after the talks, President Clinton tried to dispel any hint of a split, declaring: "Those who would try to drive a wedge between Israel and the United States will not succeed." But there were clear differences as Netanyahu stressed the priority of Israeli security and resisted US proposals to push the peace process forward.

WASHINGTON, DC, TUESDAY 9

Dole slips up on the campaign trail

With President Clinton struggling against a tide of allegations and rumors, Bob Dole should be cashing in. But the GOP presidential candidate seems to be practicing shooting himself in the foot.

Last week Dole told NBC he was "not certain" whether tobacco was addictive, a statement that drew ridicule even from some Republicans. It also drew media attention to the scale of funding for the Dole campaign from the tobacco industry.

This week Dole harmed his image with many African Americans by snubbing the NAACP and its leader Kweisi Mfume. Dole turned down an invitation to address the NAACP convention, saying Mfume was trying to "set me up." Mfume responded by calling Dole's record on civil rights "less than stellar." (→ July 31)

WASHINGTON, DC, TUESDAY 9

Smart weapons not so smart

An official survey produced for Congress by the General Accounting Office has found that claims for the effectiveness of so-called "smart" weapons in the Gulf War were exaggerated. The full survey, which took four years to complete, is secret; but an unclassified summary has been released. It says that accounts of the accuracy of such weapons as Tomahawk missiles and laser-guided bombs were "overstated, misleading, inconsistent with the best available data or unverifiable."

THE HAGUE, THURSDAY 11

Serb leaders declared fugitives

The war crimes tribunal at The Hague has issued warrants for the arrest of the Bosnian Serb leaders Radovan Karadzic and Ratko Mladic. This makes the two men international fugitives from justice and will increase pressure on the NATO forces in Bosnia to take action against them. (→ July 19)

PARIS, WEDNESDAY 10

The fall look is luxuriant and ultraslender

The twin notes of the fall haute couture shows this week are luxury and sleekness. Gianfranco Ferre, presenting his final collection for Dior, offered both opulent, shimmering, Indian-inspired gowns for the curvaceous and tailored suits for the tall and slender. Karl Lagerfeld at Chanel emphasized thinness in his use of the body stocking under long satin gowns and Chinese-embroidered coats.

Claudia Schiffer for Yves Saint Laurent.

Nadia Auermann models for Lacroix.

Linda Evangelista models for Lacroix.

Karl Lagerfeld (center) employs the new breed of ultrathin supermodel to reinterpret the flapper-girl look for Chanel.

S	M	T	W	T	F	S
	1	2	3	4	5	6
7	8	9	10	11	12	13
14	15	16	17	18	19	20
21	22	23	24	25	26	27
28	29	30	31			

Denver, 14
The Oklahoma bombing trial begins today; the defendants are former US Army soldiers Timothy McVeigh and Terry Nichols.

London, 15
The Prince and Princess of Wales are granted a preliminary divorce in court; the final decree will follow in six weeks' time. (→ August 28)

Fort Lee, NJ, 15
Microsoft and NBC launch a new 24-hour cable news service, with an on-line component, to rival CNN.

Washington, DC, 15
TV host Kathie Lee Gifford, attacked earlier in the year because her line of clothing was being produced with child labor, addresses a garment-industry summit on the topic.

Little Rock, 15
Governor Jim Guy Tucker resigns from office because of his recent Whitewater conviction and is replaced by Republican Mike Huckabee.

New York, 15
The Dow Jones index plunges by 160 points, the fourth largest drop ever in one day.

Washington, DC, 15
The antigay Defense of Marriage Act, passed in the House of Representatives, enters the Senate. (→ September 5)

Moscow, 15
President Boris Yeltsin abruptly cancels a Kremlin meeting with visiting Vice President Al Gore, announcing less than an hour before the session that he has decided to go on vacation. (→ August 9)

New York, 18
Scientists announce findings that the Earth's inner core spins faster than the crust, like a planet within a planet.

Washington, DC, 19
The House of Representatives adopts a welfare reform bill that could make the most sweeping welfare policy changes since the New Deal. (→ July 29)

Sarajevo, 19
Bosnian Serb leader Radovan Karadzic resigns from all public office after tough negotiations with US envoy Richard Holbrooke and Serb leaders in Belgrade.

NEW YORK, FRIDAY 19

Terrorism suspected in TWA disaster

The recovery crew pulls wreckage from the 120-ft-deep seas off the Long Island coast.

Investigators are still searching today for a clue to the catastrophe that struck TWA Flight 800 two days ago. The Boeing 747 jumbo jet exploded at 8:45 p.m. on July 17 shortly after taking off from New York's JFK International Airport. Many witnesses saw the burning fragments of the aircraft plunge into the Atlantic off Long Island.

The TWA flight was bound for Paris with 228 people on board—210 passengers and 18 crew. There are no survivors. Among those killed were a party of 16 high school students from Montoursville, Pennsylvania, accompanied by three adults. The mayor of Montoursville, John Dori, said: "The whole town is in mourning."

Sonar equipment has located wreckage from the plane more than 120 ft under the surface off the coast of Long Island, but the search for evidence is being hampered by fog, wind, and choppy seas. More than 100 bodies have been retrieved. Divers are preparing to search for the flight recorders, which may throw light on the cause of the tragedy.

Investigators have identified three possible origins for the devastating explosion—a bomb, a missile, or mechanical failure. The most likely explanation is a terrorist bomb planted on board. But some eyewitnesses claim to have seen a streak of light heading toward the plane, suggesting a missile attack. Alternatively, an engine fault might have ignited the plane's fuel tanks. The Boeing 747 has, however, a superlative track record for mechanical safety.

President Clinton yesterday advised against speculation on possible terrorist involvement. "Let's wait until we get the facts, and let's remember the families," he said. (→ July 25)

New Jersey, Sunday 14. The latest attempt to market professional soccer in the US seems to be working. The Major Soccer League's first All-Star Game drew 78,416 spectators to the Giants Stadium. Homegrown US players such as Alexi Lalas (far right) mix with imports such as Carlos Valderrama of Colombia (third from right).

WASHINGTON, DC, WED. 17

Primary suspect finally owns up

Primary Colors *author Joe Klein.*

The "Anonymous" author of the best-selling political satire *Primary Colors* was unmasked today as *Newsweek* columnist Joe Klein. Always a prime suspect, Klein once said: "For God's sake, definitely, I didn't write it." Now, trapped by a handwriting expert hired by the *Washington Post*, he has owned up. The book has sold more than one million copies. (→ July 26)

Olympics open with pomp and emotion

Lucid breaks US space record

NASA astronaut Shannon Lucid today set a new US record for space endurance, spending her 115th consecutive day aboard the Russian space station Mir. It is 53-year-old Lucid's fifth space flight.

Lucid was due to return to Earth in two weeks' time, but as the space shuttle is grounded with technical problems, she may have to remain in orbit for another two months. Asked how she feels about her lengthy confinement in outer space, she says she misses "junk food" and "feeling the wind and the sun." (→ September 19)

A highlight of the opening ceremony—a giant light show with blown-up silhouettes of athletes in classical Grecian-style poses.

Astronaut Shannon Lucid, age 53.

Muhammad Ali's lighting of the Olympic torch was the emotional climax of the opening.

The Centennial Olympics opened in Atlanta, Georgia, this evening with a ceremony second to none in the history of the games.

Some 11,000 athletes from 197 nations, plus 8,000 other performers, contributed to the overwhelming spectacle—as well as around 5,000 fireworks and a fleet of chrome trucks. High points included Gladys Knight singing "Georgia On My Mind" and a recording of a speech by Atlanta's famous son, Martin Luther King Jr. At one stage, massive silhouettes of athletes were projected onto a screen, resembling a Grecian frieze.

The opening ceremony astonished with its sheer size, but it was the courage of a single individual that provided the most unforgettable moment of the evening. Muhammad Ali, once the greatest boxer in the world, proudly overcame the ravages of Parkinson's disease to light the Olympic flame. To many, he seemed to represent the true spirit of the Olympic dream. (→ July 27)

Los Angeles, Thursday 18. The Lakers sign Shaquille O'Neal in a $120-million, seven-year deal—and instantly raise ticket prices, some by 100 percent.

Hotel bombing crowns a week of renewed violence

In the early hours of this morning, Northern Ireland suffered its first terrorist bombing in two years, the culmination of a week of mounting sectarian violence.

A Catholic couple were holding their wedding celebration at the Killyhevlin Hotel in Enniskillen, County Fermanagh, when a telephone warning was received at 11:40 p.m. The last guests had just cleared the building when a 1,200 lb bomb exploded. It devastated the hotel and destroyed more than 20 cars. Forty people were taken to hospital, most with minor injuries.

The IRA denied carrying out the bombing; a breakaway Republican group is suspected. There are fears that loyalists might respond by ending their own cease-fire.

July

NEW YORK, THURSDAY 25
New clues found in TWA crash investigation

Analysis of the cockpit voice recording from TWA Flight 800 has revealed the presence of a brief noise immediately before the tape ended and the aircraft crashed. The recovery yesterday of the voice recorder and the flight data recorder—the so-called black boxes—is providing aviation experts with new leads in attempting to solve the mystery of TWA Flight 800's sudden disappearance off the coast of Long Island.

A similar noise was heard on Pam Am Flight 103, shortly before it was blown out of the sky by a bomb in December 1988 while flying over Lockerbie, Scotland. This, and the absence of any vocal warning on the flight recorder, reinforces the theory that a bomb is responsible for the downing of TWA Flight 800.

President Clinton has announced wide-ranging measures to increase aircraft security, acknowledging that while they would increase expense and inconvenience, "the safety and security of the American people must be our first priority." (→ July 26)

SOUTHEAST CHINA, TUESDAY 23
China mobilizes to hold back river

In a desperate attempt to hold back the waters of the flooded Yangtze River, hundreds of thousands of soldiers and workers are being mobilized to plug leaks in embankments. Rainfall of unusual severity has caused flooding in nine provinces, killing more than 850 people.

Holding back the Yangtze has become a national priority, with more than 600,000 people deployed to watch for cracks in the dikes and to fill holes made by snakes and rats. An official at Flood Control Headquarters in the city of Wuhan said: "We are guarding the banks with our lives. This is a critical moment."

The US is leading an international relief program to provide aid to the stricken provinces. Water purifiers, plastic sheeting, and blankets are being sent to the flooded regions.

Aid workers from the Red Cross deliver medicine to flood victims in Hubei province.

JAKARTA, INDONESIA, SUNDAY 21
Jackson makes human rights appeal

Jesse Jackson: Fighting for workers' rights.

Reverend Jesse Jackson is touring Indonesia to dramatize complaints of abuses by US-owned companies. During his visit he met Indonesian pro-democracy leader Megawati Sukarnoputri, and both declared themselves allies in the battle to protect the rights of workers in Third World countries. Jackson preached two sermons in Jakarta churches, telling the congregations: "The rich are exploiting the poor, but the Christian must defend the poor."

New York, Monday 22. Rhett Butler may have said, "Frankly my dear, I don't give a damn," but *New York* magazine has named *Gone with the Wind* the most commercially successful film in the history of motion pictures. Second place goes to the musical, *The Sound of Music*.

DENVER, MONDAY 22
Clinton tough on deadbeat parents

President Clinton promised today to make life tough for deadbeat parents who fail to pay child support. "No one should be able to escape the responsibility of bringing a child into this world," the president said.

New measures proposed by President Clinton include making it a felony to hold back support payments for a child in another state, and displaying "wanted" posters of deadbeat parents in post offices and on the Internet.

ATLANTA, SATURDAY 27

Terrorist bomb rocks Atlanta—two dead

Police disperse the crowd in the wake of the bomb blast in Centennial Park.

Paramedics administer first aid to victims of the bombing: One person was killed outright, another subsequently died of a heart attack.

The harmony of the Olympic Games was devastated by an explosion during a concert in the Centennial Olympic Park at 1:25 a.m. today. The bomb, which was placed near a sound tower, left two people dead, injuring 111 more. A warning call was made 18 minutes before the blast, and officials say the caller's voice had the characteristics of a white US male. This has led the FBI to believe the explosion was the result of domestic terrorism.

Security at the Games has been stepped up, as an army of state and federal agents search for clues to track down those responsible for the outrage. (→ July 30)

ATLANTA, SATURDAY 27

US golden girl breaks through pain barrier at Olympics

US women gymnasts have so far proved to be the stars of the Centennial Games. On Wednesday America was overwhelmed by the courage of 18-year-old Kerri Strug. Believing her vault was needed to secure a gold for the US women's team, Strug performed despite suffering a badly twisted ankle. She collapsed in pain after her landing, but the medal was won and the nation moved in a manner that will long be remembered.

Although Irish swimmer Michelle Smith eclipsed Janet Evans, the US swimming team has harvested a rich crop of gold medals.

The track and field events got underway toward the end of the week. In the men's 100 meters, US hope Dennis Mitchell was beaten into fourth place, but Gail Devers won gold for the US in the women's 100 meters. (→ July 31)

Kerri Strug is carried to the medal ceremony by the US gymnastics coach, Bela Karolyi.

SRI LANKA, WEDNESDAY 24

Tamil Tigers unleash new offensive

Resurgent Tamil Tigers have blown up a crowded commuter train outside Sri Lanka's capital, Colombo, killing more than 60 people and wounding nearly 450 others. The attack was part of a new terrorist campaign instigated by the Tigers to reassert their authority over the Jaffna Peninsula, following their expulsion by government forces last year.

Yesterday a government army camp was overrun by the Tigers after a ferocious mortar bombardment. According to rebel sources, only a handful of troops escaped from a garrison of over 1,200. Although government forces have now recaptured the camp at Mullaitivu, the Tamil Tigers have proved their ability to mount conventional operations.

S	M	T	W	T	F	S
	1	2	3	4	5	6
7	8	9	10	11	12	13
14	15	16	17	18	19	20
21	22	23	24	25	26	27
28	29	30	31			

Los Angeles, 29
Baseball's Tommy Lasorda, Dodgers manager for nearly two decades, retires at age 68 because of heart trouble.

Washington, DC, 29
President Clinton announces an agreement with TV executives that guarantees three hours of educational programing a week for children.

Jakarta, Indonesia, 30
The Indonesian military threatens to shoot rioters on sight amid rumors of fresh disturbances in the capital.

Washington, DC, 30
Data released today shows that consumer confidence in the US has hit a six-year high as the economy continues to grow.

Moscow, 30
Pravda, the newspaper founded by Lenin 84 years ago, bows to market forces and is relaunched as a down-market tabloid.

Dallas, 30
In a mail survey, Reform party members choose Ross Perot and former Colorado governor Richard Lamm to compete for the presidential nomination next month. (→ August 18)

Smithtown, NY, 30
Jim Kallstrom, the FBI agent in charge of the TWA Flight 800 crash inquiry, admits that there is still no hard evidence to confirm investigators' theory that the plane was blown up by a bomb. (→ August 26)

Washington, DC, 31
President Clinton announces he will sign the Welfare Reform bill that will end the 60-year-old federal promise of open-ended assistance to every poor family.

Tijuana, Mexico, 31
The Mexican Congress opens a special session to discuss the biggest reforms to the country's political system in 60 years. Changes include diluting the power of the president and the ruling party, and electing a mayor for Mexico City.

Arusha, Tanzania, 31
African leaders agree to impose a total economic blockade on Burundi after last week's coup, to press for a return to constitutional rule. (→ August 6)

ATLANTA, TUESDAY 30
Bombing hero becomes a suspect

Richard Jewell, the 33-year-old security guard who was credited with spotting the bomb.

Richard Jewell, the security guard hailed as a hero in the Centennial Olympic Park bombing, is being questioned by the FBI. Officials say that Jewell, who was credited with spotting the bomb, may have planted the device in order to set himself up as a hero. Jewell made several TV appearances following the bombing, but video footage from surveillance cameras in the park contradicts some of his statements. (→ August 5)

Barbados, Tuesday 30. Claudette Colbert, star of more than 60 films, dies at age 93. She won the 1934 Academy Award for her star role alongside Clark Gable in *It Happened One Night*.

PARIS, TUESDAY 30
Leading nations meet to target terrorism

The world's leading political powers met in Paris today to set measures for combatting terrorism. A wave of terrorist attacks around the world, most recently in Atlanta and Dhahran, prompted the one-day meeting for the group of seven leading industrial nations and Russia. The recommendations from the meeting include tightening and standardizing border checks, simplifying extradition rules, and investigating charitable groups thought to back terrorists.

LOS ANGELES, WEDNESDAY 31
Stay upbeat, Dole tells Hollywood

Presidential candidate Bob Dole today urged Hollywood to produce more uplifting movies, in a softer sequel to his 1995 speech where he slammed the industry for producing "depravity drenched in violence and sex." Dole told a group of 20th Century Fox executives that "respectability is good business," and singled out *Babe*, *Braveheart*, and *Apollo 13* for approval. Although his speech was warmly received, critics point out that attacking Hollywood is a politician's easy ticket to front-page coverage.

Bob Dole with his wife Elizabeth, after addressing a group of Hollywood executives.

ATLANTA, WEDNESDAY 31
US chases medal record as Olympic Games continue

Michael Johnson, men's 200-meters record holder, winning the 400 meters on Monday.

The Atlanta Games continued this week, shaken but not deterred after Saturday's bomb attack. The US medal count reached 51 today, but it was Ethiopian Atuna Roba who stole the show, winning the women's marathon in 2 hours, 26 minutes, and 5 seconds in her first major event.

On Monday, fans who turned out for Carl Lewis's swan song were not disappointed as the 35-year-old took gold in the long jump. Michael Johnson completed part of his campaign to become the first man to win the 200 meters and the 400 meters at the same Olympics by winning the 400 meters. And the US women's softball team captured gold after defeating China 3-1 on Tuesday. (→ August 4)

Carl Lewis—the "world's greatest athlete"—winning his fourth consecutive gold medal in the long jump, and his ninth Olympic gold.

GENEVA, TUESDAY 30
Nuclear powers discuss ban while China sets off "last" blast

China conducted what it says will be its last nuclear test yesterday, at the same time as negotiators from 61 countries were meeting in Geneva to complete a global test ban agreement.

China, the last nuclear power to halt testing, said that it would impose a moratorium following Monday's test in the northwestern Xinjiang region. The announcement was welcomed by Western nuclear powers and Russia, who have all agreed to a compromise text of the Comprehensive Test Ban Treaty under discussion in Geneva.

Objections by China and India may delay an agreement, however. China disagrees with proposals for on-site inspection and verification, while India is refusing to sign unless the five main nuclear powers commit to full disarmament. (→ September 10)

SOUTH AFRICA, WED. 31
Rush hour stampede at train station kills 15

Fifteen people have been killed and more than 50 injured in a stampede at a train station that started when security guards used electric prods to control crowds. The incident occurred in Tembisa township, 20 miles northeast of Johannesburg, during this morning's rush hour. Outraged youths then set fire to the ticket office and stoned riot police as they arrived.

Witnesses at the scene say train passengers arrived at the station to find the ticket office shut, and attempted to board the train without tickets. There was crushing as people tried to force their way past the control point, and private security guards—hired to crack down on nonpaying commuters—used electric shock batons to turn back passengers without tickets.

The government has ordered an urgent inquiry into what President Nelson Mandela has called "a national tragedy," with special attention to be paid to allegations of "unnecessary force" by the security guards.

London, Wednesday 31. Crowds turned out to Kew Gardens to see—and smell—the rare titan arum as it bloomed for the first time in 33 years, giving off its distinctive odor of rotting fish.

S	M	T	W	T	F	S
				1	2	3
4	5	6	7	8	9	10
11	12	13	14	15	16	17
18	19	20	21	22	23	24
25	26	27	28	29	30	31

Washington, DC, 2
US intelligence experts report finding evidence, partially through satellite observations, of 11 terrorist training camps in Iran.

Atlanta, 5
Richard Jewell, the security guard named as a suspect in the Atlanta bomb inquiry, threatens to sue the FBI. (→ September 22)

Washington, DC, 5
President Clinton signs a bill that would penalize companies from any country that invest in oil projects in Iran and Libya.

Chicago, 5
Bob Dole introduces a Reaganesque tax package, with a 15 percent tax cut for all, as the new centerpiece of his presidential campaign.

Rome, 5
Erich Priebke, the former German Nazi SS Captain freed by a court in Rome despite admitting to a part in a wartime massacre of civilians, is rearrested at Germany's request.

Burundi, 6
Tanzania becomes the first country to enforce the embargo against Burundi by blocking oil at the landlocked country's border. (→ August 20)

Washington, DC, 8
The Internet system America Online crashes after maintenance work in suburban Washington, DC, leaving six million users around the world out in the cold for 18 hours.

Chicago, 8
A University of Chicago study shows that states that allow people to carry concealed handguns have a diminished violent crime rate.

Atlanta, 9
Pepsi is being sued by a 21-year-old business student, John Leonard, who claims they owe him a Harrier jump jet, offered in an ad to collectors of seven million container points.

Deaths
August 2. Michel Debre, former French prime minister, at age 84.

August 9. Sir Frank Whittle, British inventor of the jet engine, at age 89, in Columbia, Maryland.

MOSCOW, FRIDAY 9

Yeltsin inauguration prompts fresh health fears

Boris Yeltsin, showing obvious signs of poor health, is sworn in as president on Friday.

A frail-looking Boris Yeltsin was inaugurated today as Russia's first democratically elected leader in the post-Communist era.

The president, who has not been seen in public since June 26, spent only 16 minutes on stage, performing his duties with obvious difficulty. His speech was slurred during the oath of office, and he delivered no inaugural remarks to the 3,000 dignitaries who watched in silence.

What should have been a historic celebration was further overshadowed by events in Chechnya, where a rebel offensive in Grozny entered its fourth day. More than 120 Russian soldiers were reported dead and 400 wounded in the worst fighting since 1994. (→ September 6)

LITTLE ROCK, THURSDAY 1

Clinton celebrates acquittal of Arkansas bankers

White House officials have described Bill Clinton as "jubilant" over the news of the acquittal of two Arkansas bankers in Little Rock yesterday.

Herby Branscum Jr. and Robert M. Hill were cleared on four charges of fraud and conspiracy. It was alleged that the two men defrauded their own bank to help Mr. Clinton's 1990 gubernatorial campaign. The verdict is seen as a setback for prosecutor Kenneth Starr, who won guilty verdicts in May against President Clinton's former partners in the Whitewater real-estate venture.

Arkansas banker Herby Branscum Jr. (left).

ATLANTA, SATURDAY 3

Muhammad Ali receives honorary gold to replace 1960 medal

Muhammad Ali, during his second emotional appearance at the Atlanta Games.

The former world champion boxer Muhammad Ali tonight received an honorary gold medal to replace one that he threw away in the 1960s in protest against racism. Ali, then Cassius Clay, hurled the medal he won at the Rome 1960 Olympics into a river after he was refused entry to a white-run restaurant in Kentucky and harassed by a gang of white bikers.

Ali, now 54 and suffering from Parkinson's disease, was awarded the medal by Juan Antonio Samaranch, the president of the International Olympic Committee, during halftime of the basketball finals.

Meteorite yields clues to life on Mars

Scientists are examining pieces of a Martian meteorite for evidence of early life on Mars.

NASA officials announced today that US scientists have found signs in a Martian meteorite that a primitive form of life may have existed on Mars more than the billion years ago.

A NASA statement said that US scientists had discovered circumstantial evidence of early life forms in a Martian meteorite that landed on earth 13,000 years ago, and was recovered in Antarctica in 1984. NASA administrator Daniel Goldin stressed, "We are not talking about 'little green men.' These are extremely small, single-cell structures."

President Clinton said the news was "as awe inspiring as can be imagined," and hailed it as a vindication of the US space program. (→ October 31)

Biescas, Spain, Thursday 8. At least 100 people are feared dead and 200 injured after a flooded river burst its banks last night and surged through a holiday campsite in the Pyrenees.

Senator views killer's execution

Oklahoma state senator Brooks Douglass and his sister Leslie Frizzell today plan to watch the execution at Oklahoma State Penitentiary of one of the men who killed their parents 17 years ago. Steven Hatch, 43, was sentenced to death in 1980 for his part in murdering Richard and Marilyn Douglass while their two children watched. Brooks Douglass, now 32, drafted the new state law that allows victims' relatives to view executions.

Ex-Nazi cleared on war crimes charge

Former Nazi SS Captain Erich Priebke was freed today after a military court in Rome ruled he was only following orders when he took part in the massacre of 335 Italian civilians during World War II.

Relatives of victims screamed and wept as the verdict was announced, and blocked Priebke from leaving the courtroom for four hours. Shimon Samuels of the Simon Wiesenthal Center, which helped to hunt down Priebke in Argentina, said bitterly after the verdict: "Italy endorses crimes against humanity." (→ August 5)

Former Nazi SS officer Erich Priebke.

Atlanta, Sunday 4. Josia Thugwane becomes the first black South African to win an Olympic gold medal with his victory in the men's marathon. His countrymen cheered news of his win at home, and President Nelson Mandela dubbed him "South Africa's golden boy."

US tops medal tally as Games end

As the men's marathon on Sunday brought the Atlanta Olympics to an end, the US maintained its top position in the medal count with 101 medals—43 of which are gold.

To the end, the Games provided enthralling sporting images: on Friday Michael Johnson smashed his own 200-meter world record by 0.34 seconds to become the first man ever to win both the 200-meter and 400-meter races in the same Olympics. The US men's 4 x 100-meters relay team was outshone by Canada—anchored by the 100-meters winner Donovan Bailey—but the women's 4 x 100-meters relay team won their fourth straight gold in the event. And the Dream Team carried off their gold medal, as expected, on Saturday after the final against Yugoslavia.

August

Istanbul, 11
Turkey agrees to a multibillion dollar natural gas deal with Iran, and insists that it does not defy US sanctions against trading with Iran.

Oregon, 11
A judge orders Oregon to offer health insurance to the partners of gay state employees, on the same basis as that provided in heterosexual unions.

New York, 11
Willie King receives a three-year prison sentence for mugging the 94-year-old mother of Mafia boss Vincent Gigante. King owned up after discovering who his victim was.

Louisville, KY, 12
Golfer Mark Brooks wins the 78th US PGA tournament and $430,000 prize money.

Los Angeles, 12
Rodney King, awarded $3.8 million after being beaten by LA police in 1991, has filed a lawsuit against his former lawyer, Steven Lerman, accusing him of mismanaging the money.

Virginia, 13
The Virginia Zoo's hippopotamus, Nyla, age 32, dies of a bowel obstruction caused by a racquetball that a visitor had apparently thrown into the animal's pen.

New York, 14
NASA scientists believe that Europa, a moon of the planet Jupiter, is covered in frozen water, and might contain evidence of life.

London, 15
Princess Diana takes out an injunction against a photographer, who is banned from going within 300 yards of her.

Indianapolis, 15
Andre Agassi is expelled from the RCA Championships for swearing at an umpire.

Philippines, 16
A British student and two Filipino mountain climbers are killed when a volcano on the Philippine island of Negros erupts without warning.

Deaths
August 11. Rafael Kubelik, former conductor of the Chicago Symphony Orchestra, at age 82.

Lebed attacks Moscow leadership

Given sweeping powers by President Yeltsin to end the war in Chechnya, Russian security advisor Alexander Lebed has demanded the dismissal of the newly appointed interior minister, Anatoli Kulikov. A former general, Kulikov was one of the men responsible for sending Russian troops into Chechnya, and Lebed regards him as an inept "Napoleon" bent on death and destruction.

This demand is typical brinkmanship from the pugnacious Lebed, who believes Russia cannot afford to continue its costly occupation of Chechnya. Russian troops continue to suffer at the hands of the rebels, although Lebed remains confident that he can broker a face-saving peace. (→ August 23)

Peace negotiator Alexander Lebed.

Professors shot by student over thesis

An engineering student was today accused of killing three professors at San Diego State University because of problems with his thesis. Police say Frederick Davidson, 36, was due to defend his master's thesis at a meeting on Thursday, but opened fire on his faculty adviser, Chen Liang, and two professors instead. Davidson allegedly fired 20 rounds at the professors, but let three students in the room escape.

Girls' bodies found in house of horror

Marc Dutroux (right) is arrested and led away by Belgian police.

Belgian police dug up the bodies of two girls and an adult today in the garden of a house owned by 39-year-old Marc Dutroux. Yesterday police found two other girls shackled in an underground chamber in the house. Both had been sexually abused.

The dead girls have been identified as Melissa Russo and Julie Lejeune, both age eight, who had been missing for 14 months. They apparently starved to death while Dutroux was in police custody on another matter.

Dutroux was a known pedophile. Police twice visited his house during

Melissa Russo (left) and Julie Lejune.

the search for the missing girls, but did not find them. Convicted for pedophile offenses in 1989, Dutroux served only three years of a 13-year sentence. (→ August 21)

England, Tuesday 13. An executive Learjet overshot a runway on the outskirts of London during landing and crashed into a van on a nearby highway. The three people on the plane escaped with minor injuries, as did the van driver, who said, "I am happy to be alive."

DHERINIA, CYPRUS, SUNDAY 11

Bikers' protest ends in death

Troops from a UN peace-keeping force were unable to prevent the latest upsurge in violence on the Mediterranean island of Cyprus that has left one dead and 50 wounded.

Greek Cypriot Tassos Isaac was beaten to death, in one of the worst clashes for years between the Greek and Turkish communities on the island. Hundreds of Greek Cypriot motorcyclists had defied a government order to cancel a mass protest against Turkey's continuing occupation of northern Cyprus. Fighting broke out as the bikers attempted to penetrate into the Turkish-held areas.

US, August. Topping the box office this month is *A Time to Kill*, starring Sandra Bullock and Matthew McConaughey, and based on John Grisham's novel.

ROCHESTER, NY, MON. 12

Neighbor admits killing missing girl

The two-year, nationwide search for four-year-old Kali Poulton has ended with the arrest of Mark Christie, who lived only 100 yards away from her home. Kali's decomposed body was discovered in a water tank where Christie worked. The search for Kali, who was abducted on May 23, 1994, ended when Christie's wife of three weeks turned him in after Christie admitted to the crime during an argument.

Greek Cypriot bikers drive to the border zone to confront the Turkish Cypriot authorities.

SEOUL, SOUTH KOREA, THURSDAY 15

Students fight for reunification

Backed by helicopters, South Korean riot police today stormed a university in Seoul for the second day running, to end demonstrations by students calling for reunification with communist North Korea. Students hurled stones and gas bombs at the police, who replied with volleys of tear gas, which dispersed the students to the shelter of campus buildings. Nearly 1,000 students were cornered in a science department block, but they kept the police at bay by threatening to set off a series of explosions.

The police had originally decided to enter the university to stop the protesters from marching to the border village of Panmunjom, about 25 miles away, to meet North Koreans for a joint rally. (→August 20)

SAN DIEGO, THURSDAY 15

Republican nominee Dole stresses trust in US

In his acceptance speech for the Republican party nomination yesterday, Bob Dole made the standard promises to balance the budget and cut taxes. He refused to jump on the right-wing bandwagon, however, emphasizing instead the need for "inclusion" and "compassion" in government, which, he said, depended on the trust of the American people.

As in any well-managed television event, dissenting voices were kept in the background, and the controversial issue of abortion—which had threatened to cause acrimony between pro-life and pro-choice wings of the party—was almost never mentioned by podium speakers.

The success of the convention owed much to the choice of former rival Jack Kemp as vice-presidential running mate, and also to the presence of Bob Dole's charismatic wife, Elizabeth, who left the stage to walk among the delegates and talk about the "man I love."

Bob and Elizabeth Dole wave to a cheering crowd at the Republican party convention in San Diego.

S	M	T	W	T	F	S
				1	2	3
4	5	6	7	8	9	10
11	12	13	14	15	16	17
18	19	20	21	22	23	24
25	26	27	28	29	30	31

Washington, DC, 18
Ross Perot becomes Reform party candidate for the presidency, brushing aside a challenge from former Colorado governor Richard Lamm.

Woburn, England, 18
Californian golfer Emilee Klein wins the British Women's Open, seven shots ahead of fellow US golfers Penny Hammel and Amy Alcott.

Belfast, Northern Ireland, 18
IRA terrorist Jimmy Smyth, who escaped from the Maze prison in Belfast in 1983, is extradited from the US and will now serve the remaining 15 years of his 20-year sentence.

Canberra, Australia, 19
Sixty police and demonstrators are hurt in clashes outside Parliament House prior to Prime Minister John Howard's announcement of $3 billion-worth of cuts in the coalition government's first budget.

Seoul, South Korea, 20
Korean riot police clear protestors from Seoul university in a dawn raid. The students are demanding that US troops withdraw from Korea and that North and South Korea be reunited.

Burundi, 20
Burundi's military leader, Major Pierre Buyoya, dismisses three key military officers in a bid for international approval and an end to trade sanctions. (→ September 5)

Washington, DC, 20
Drug use among US teenagers has increased by 78 percent since 1992, according to the National Household Survey on Drug Control Policy.

Little Rock, 20
Susan McDougal is sentenced to two years in jail and three years probation in the Whitewater case. (→ September 5)

Cape Town, 21
National Party leader F. W. de Klerk tells the Truth and Reconciliation Commission that he prayed for forgiveness for apartheid.

Hamburg, 22
Gary Lauck, US neo-Nazi, is jailed for four years after being found guilty of the illegal supply to Germany of racist hate propaganda.

NEW YORK, SUNDAY 18
Clinton celebrates 50th birthday at star-studded event

Chelsea Clinton helps her father to blow out the 50 birthday candles while Hillary looks on.

New York's Radio City Music Hall was tonight the setting for the most lavish presidential birthday party since Marilyn Monroe serenaded John F. Kennedy in 1962. President Clinton, age 50, had singers from the five decades of his life to entertain him, from Tony Bennett to Shania Twain. Whoopi Goldberg hosted the show, which was broadcast to fund-raising venues across the US.

President Clinton needs to regain the initiative after last week's triumphal Republican convention. This week he signs new healthcare legislation and a welfare reform bill that will end the universal safety-net for the poor created 60 years ago by the New Deal. Although controversial, these measures are likely to increase the president's chances of reelection.

PARIS, SATURDAY 24
French celebrities back black protestors

Riot police stormed the Saint Bernard church in the Goutte d'Or district of Paris yesterday, evicting 300 African immigrants, including ten who had been on hunger strike for 50 days. Even though many have lived in the country for years, the immigrants face expulsion from France under tough immigration laws passed in 1993.

President Chirac issued the order to send in riot police despite popular support for the immigrants. Notable French celebrities, including actress Emmanuelle Béart, had gathered at the church, hoping to prevent the expulsion, and several thousand protestors marched through Paris last night. (→ August 25)

London, Wednesday 21. An exact replica of Shakespeare's Globe Theatre opened tonight on the site of the original, fulfilling the dream of late US director Sam Wanamaker, who long fought for the project.

Riot police fight their way through demonstrators outside Saint Bernard church.

SOUTH AFRICA, MONDAY 19
Fresh shooting sparks panic

A German business executive, Erich Ellmer, was shot dead outside his home in Johannesburg yesterday, in an attempted kidnapping that went wrong. The murder highlights the increasing levels of violence and drug-related crime in South Africa. With the police apparently impotent, people are increasingly turning to armed vigilantes to counter the crime wave. A Muslim vigilante group publicly murdered a drug dealer in the Cape Flats area of Cape Town last week.

Belgian pedophile hunt extends abroad

Belgian police are today seeking help from other forces in Europe to track down the pedophile ring thought to be associated with Marc Dutroux, arrested for the killing of two young girls. At present the police have no firm leads, as they are heavily dependent on Dutroux's confession. He denies killing the girls, Melissa Russo and Julie Lejune, claiming they were murdered by an accomplice whom he subsequently killed in a fit of rage.

The police are also investigating how Dutroux, a 39-year-old electrician of modest means, managed to acquire 11 properties in Belgium. This suggests that he has received money from elsewhere, backing his claim that he abducted children in order to sell them abroad. (→ September 3)

Relations mourn at the coffins of Melissa Russo and Julie Lejune.

Mother gorilla is hailed as a hero

A three-year-old boy left the hospital today with only minor injuries thanks to the maternal behavior of an ape named Binti Jua. Meanwhile, at Brookfield Zoo in Illinois. Binti Jua, mother of a 16-month-old gorilla named Koola, was basking in the limelight as fans arrived to pay homage to the US's latest animal hero.

Last Friday Binti Jua amazed onlookers when she carried the boy to safety after he had accidentally fallen into the rock-strewn gorilla pen.

Philippine leader agrees deal to end rebellion

President Fidel Ramos met with the Muslim chairman of the Moro National Liberation Front, Nur Misuari, on the island of Mindanao yesterday, where they agreed to end the war that has been fought there for 26 years, claiming more than 150,000 lives. The two leaders discussed details of a complex agreement that is designed to give some degree of Moro autonomy when it is finalized on September 2.

Russia ends bombardment of Grozny and signs cease-fire

As the cease-fire takes effect, a resident of Grozny walks through the battered remains of the Chechen capital.

After days of ferocious bombardment, Russian guns fell silent in Grozny at 9 a.m. today. The cease-fire was engineered by national security chief Alexander Lebed yesterday. Under the agreement, Russian troops will pull back from positions near Chechen strongholds. This will leave the Chechen guerrillas in control of most of Grozny, which they captured from Russian forces after an audacious assault on August 6.

Lebed's concessions to the rebels reflect his belief that Russia cannot win a military victory. His approach is popular with the war-weary Russian people, but he has been criticized by President Yeltsin. (→ August 31)

New York, Wednesday 21. The flamboyant Chicago Bulls basketball star, Dennis Rodman, signs copies of his new book, *Bad as I Wanna Be*, sporting a wedding dress, a blond wig, and bright red lipstick.

S	M	T	W	T	F	S
				1	2	3
4	5	6	7	8	9	10
11	12	13	14	15	16	17
18	19	20	21	22	23	24
25	26	27	28	29	30	31

Charleston, SC, 25
Four women enroll at The Citadel, South Carolina's previously all-male military college.

Washington, DC, 25
US intelligence reports claim that China is helping Pakistan build medium-range missiles, capable of delivering nuclear warheads.

Paris, 25
The French authorities allow 45 of the 220 illegal immigrants detained at the end of the Saint Bernard church siege last week to stay in the country.

Pretoria, South Africa, 27
Former South African police colonel Eugene de Kock is convicted of six murders committed during the apartheid era. (→ September 18)

Havana, 27
Rogue financier Robert Vesco, who fled the US 25 years ago facing fraud charges, has been sentenced to 13 years in prison by a Cuban court for marketing a drug without the approval of the government.

Jerusalem, 28
Palestinian leader Yasir Arafat calls for a campaign of civil disobedience against the Israeli authorities following the demolition of an Arab community center. (→ September 4)

New York, 28
Fifteen people are arrested at an Orthodox synagogue in Queens, charged with operating a clandestine casino four nights a week.

Washington, DC, 29
The US Commerce Department issues figures showing strong growth of the US economy at 4.8 percent annually.

South Africa, 31
Nelson Mandela confirms that he is having an affair with Graca Machel, the widow of Mozambique's former leader, Samora Machel.

Iraq, 31
US troops are put on standby as Iraqi troops seize the town of Irbil in the Kurdish "safe haven" in the north of Iraq. (→ September 3)

Deaths
August 27. Bernard B. Jacobs, Broadway producer and theater mogul, at age 80.

Lebed signs peace deal with Chechens

Russian National Security Advisor, Alexander Lebed, signed a peace treaty today with Chechen leader Aslan Maskhadov. After eight hours of talks, Lebed emerged from the meeting with the Chechen rebels to announce: "That is it, the war is over." The treaty, which ends nearly two years of war in which at least 30,000 people have died, is clearly a diplomatic maneuver. Russian troops will withdraw from Chechnya, but the status of the country will not be finally decided until after December 31, 2001.

Russian hardliners will claim that the treaty is a sellout to the Chechens, but Alexander Lebed has been prepared to stake his political reputation on the war's unpopularity with the Russian people. (→ September 3)

Shaking hands for peace: Aslan Maskhadov (left) and Alexander Lebed.

Moscow, Sunday 25. Russian-born swimmer Alexander Popov, who won two gold and two silver medals in Atlanta, is recovering in the hospital after being stabbed last night in a street altercation.

TWA 800 mystery continues to baffle flight experts

Investigators have concluded that the explosion aboard TWA Flight 800 was not caused by an electrical short circuit, thus ruling out one of the more common forms of mechanical failure.

The theory that the aircraft was hit by a missile was lent some credence by a snapshot taken from a Long Island restaurant at about the time of the explosion. It shows what looks like a cylinder, with one end aglow, streaking across the sky. The photograph is being examined by FBI experts.

Not in doubt, however, is the cost of the investigation, now nearing $10 million—the most expensive crash investigation ever. (→ October 12)

Korean former president faces death

A former South Korean president, Chun Doo Hwan, was today sentenced to death, convicted of masterminding a military coup in 1979 and ordering a massacre of civilian demonstrators in the city of Kwangju the following year. His co-defendant and successor as president, Roh Tae Woo, was jailed for 22 years for his role in the coup.

Other South Korean business and military leaders received lesser sentences, as part of current President Kim Young Sam's campaign to "right the wrongs of history." Relatives of those killed in the Kwangju massacre cheered at the news of Chun's death sentence. However, it is thought likely that he will benefit from a presidential pardon.

The hangar where remnants of TWA flight 800 are being pieced together.

CHICAGO, THURSDAY 29

Clinton proclaims, "Hope is back"

President Bill Clinton's acceptance speech tonight ended the Democratic National Convention on a high note. The scandal of Clinton aide Dick Morris's resignation was put aside as the party closed ranks behind their president. Pledging to "build a bridge to the 21st century," Clinton told delegates that "hope is back in America."

The four-day build-up to the nomination had been smoothly managed. Hillary and Chelsea Clinton were given prominence to stress the Democratic commitment to family values. Jim Brady, disabled in the Reagan assassination attempt in 1981, made an emotional appearance with his wife to plead for gun controls. And wheelchair-bound Christopher Reeve made a moving appeal for aid for Americans with disabilities.

A riot of flags, balloons, and banners welcomes Bill Clinton to the convention hall.

Christopher Reeve makes an emotional speech on behalf of the disabled during the first night of the Democratic convention.

CHICAGO, THURSDAY 29

Clinton aide resigns over call-girl scandal

The man largely credited with engineering President Bill Clinton's recent political comeback has resigned today amid reports that he gave administration secrets to a prostitute. Dick Morris was named by the *Star*, a US tabloid, as hiring a $200-an-hour prostitute and allowing her to listen to a telephone call from the president. The *Star* also claims that Morris gave the prostitute a copy of a Hillary Clinton speech five days before it was delivered.

The White House refused to comment on the allegations, but in a statement President Clinton said, "Dick Morris is my friend and he is a superb political strategist."

The front cover of the Star, *which broke the news of the Dick Morris scandal.*

LONDON, WEDNESDAY 28

Royal marriage ends with a rubber stamp

The 15-year marriage of the Prince and Princess of Wales ended today at Somerset House in London, with a civil servant's stamp granting a decree absolute. The prime minister, John Major, said that there was no prospect of an early remarriage for Prince Charles, despite his continuing relationship with Camilla Parker Bowles.

The Princess of Wales, who is to be stripped of the title Her Royal Highness, began her new life as a single woman by attending a long-standing lunchtime engagement at the English National Ballet in London. Significantly, perhaps, she continued to wear her wedding and engagement rings.

TRIPOLI, LIBYA, FRIDAY 30

US bans Farrakhan from accepting gift from Libya

The US government has denied the Nation of Islam leader Louis Farrakhan permission to accept a gift of $1 billion from Libya's leader, Colonel Muammar Gadhafi, that was intended to aid black Americans.

Mr. Farrakhan, who arrived in Libya on Wednesday, accepted a $250,000 Libyan human-rights prize, even though this gift was also banned by the US. The Treasury Department's Richard Newcombe cited the belief that Libya is a "strong supporter of terrorist groups" as one of the reasons for the prohibition. Speaking at a news conference with Arab journalists,

Mr. Farrakhan condemned US sanctions against Libya, claiming that he had come to Tripoli "on behalf of black people in the United States." Before his departure, he said, "I will go across the nation stirring up not only my own people, but all those who would benefit from this gift."

S	M	T	W	T	F	S
1	2	3	4	5	6	7
8	9	10	11	12	13	14
15	16	17	18	19	20	21
22	23	24	25	26	27	28
29	30					

Mexico City, 1
President Ernesto Zedillo of Mexico denounces guerrillas in his State of the Union address, and says that the Popular Revolutionary Army will be hunted down.

Charleroi, Belgium, 3
In the Belgian child sex murder case, police find two more bodies buried in a house owned by confessed pedophile Marc Dutroux. (→ October 19)

London, 3
Rhinoceros horns worth $4 million are seized by police in London, the world's largest haul ever. Ground rhino horns are sold as a valuable aphrodisiac in the Far East.

Moscow, 3
General Lebed says the death toll in the 21-month Chechen conflict may have reached 90,000. (→ October 16)

Persian Gulf, 4
The US launches a second missile strike against Iraq, amid reports of continuing Iraqi shelling in northern Kurdish areas. (→ September 9)

Egan, MN, 4
Computer scientists say that they have found the largest prime number, with 378,632 digits.

New York, 5
Rock group The Smashing Pumpkins dominates the MTV Video Awards ceremony, taking seven awards.

New York, 5
Ramzi Ahmed Yousef is found guilty of plotting to blow up 12 airliners bound for the US. The apparent aim of the terrorist plan was to make the US reconsider its Middle East policy.

Little Rock, 5
Susan McDougal is held in contempt of court for refusing to answer questions about President Clinton in front of a grand jury. (→ September 10)

Washington, DC, 5
The Senate takes up discussion of the anti-gay Defense of Marriage Act, approved by the House 342 to 67 in August. (→ September 10)

Bujumbura, Burundi, 5
Burundi's army launches an offensive against Hutu rebel forces, trying to drive them from hills overlooking the capital.

US launches 27 missiles against Iraq

The US launched a missile strike against Iraq early this morning, in response to Iraqi incursions into Kurdish safe havens in northern Iraq during the weekend. The attack from the Gulf involved two B52 bombers and two guided-missile warships, which fired 27 cruise missiles on targets in southern Iraq. Iraqi sources said five people were killed and 19 injured.

In an address from the Oval Office after the attack, President Clinton said that he had extended one of the two Western-imposed no-fly zones in Iraq. He has also blocked a UN plan, due to take effect later this month, that would allow Iraq to sell oil for food.

Iraqi leader Saddam Hussein was defiant after the attack, declaring the allied no-fly zones "null and void," and ordering his forces to shoot down hostile aircraft patrolling the areas. Western intelligence sources say that Iraqi tanks are moving deeper into northern Kurdish areas, despite Iraq's claims that their troops are withdrawing. Last Saturday, the Iraqi military supported the Kurdish Democratic Party in capturing the city of Irbil from a rival Kurdish faction.

Most of America's allies have condemned the strike, with only Britain offering full support. But US Defense Secretary William Perry said emphatically that the US would take further action if necessary. (→ September 4)

A Tomahawk cruise missile is launched from the US destroyer Laboon in the Gulf.

Kurds fleeing from Iraqi and hostile Kurdish forces line up for water at a refugee camp.

US, Wednesday 4. The new thriller *The Crow: City of Angels*, starring Vincent Perez (right), brought the summer box office to a record-breaking close. It opened at No. 1, taking an estimated $10 million.

Seven die during visit to tragic lake

Residents of Union, South Carolina, are calling for the lake where Susan Smith killed her two sons in October 1994 to be filled in, after seven people drowned there on Saturday night.

Three adults and four children were killed when their car rolled into John D. Long Lake. The victims were part of a group of ten who had come to see the site where Ms. Smith pushed her car into the lake with her sons strapped inside. An entire family was killed in Saturday's accident— Tim Phillips, 26, his wife Angela, 22, and their three children—as well as toddler Austin Roodvoets and 29-year-old Carl White.

MOSCOW, FRIDAY 6
Yeltsin comes clean on heart operation

Only two months after his re-election as president of Russia, Boris Yeltsin yesterday admitted to the Russian people that he needs heart bypass surgery. In a TV interview, Yeltsin said he would undergo the operation before the end of the month. Today there is mounting pressure on the president to appoint a temporary replacement as fears of a power vacuum grow. (→ September 19)

Plains, GA, Sunday 1. Amy Carter, the 28-year-old daughter of former US president Jimmy Carter, married James Wentzel, 27, in a simple ceremony.

BALTIMORE, SUNDAY 1
Ravens mark NFL debut with victory

Baltimore heartily welcomed back the National Football League on Sunday with the Ravens' 19-14 win over the Oakland Raiders. Veteran quarterback Vinny Testaverde was the key to Baltimore's victory, scrambling 12 yards to set up the winning touchdown less than eight minutes from the end. The game was watched by 64,000, relishing their first taste of the NHL since the Colts left for Indianapolis 13 years ago. In another debut, new Miami Dolphins coach Jimmy Johnson watched his team beat the New England Patriots 24-10.

EREZ, ISRAEL, WEDNESDAY 4
Leaders shake hands across the divide

Netanyahu (left) and Arafat shake hands at the Erez checkpoint in the Gaza Strip.

The new Israeli prime minister, Benjamin Netanyahu, once declared that he would never meet with the Palestinian leader Yasir Arafat because he considered him a terrorist. But today the two men briefly clasped hands across a table in a gesture that might just put the Middle East peace process back on track.

The one-hour summit meeting at Erez on the Gaza border predictably failed to produce any practical moves toward agreement between the two sides. Arafat continues to call for full implementation of accords signed with the previous Israeli government. Netanyahu pointedly refuses to admit that he might be bound by previous agreements. (→ September 27)

NORTH CAROLINA, SATURDAY 7
Hurricane Fran devastates the Carolinas, leaving 12 dead

Damage along the coast near Wilmington, North Carolina, which was the largest city to feel the full force of the hurricane.

Hurricane Fran ripped through the Carolinas Thursday night and early Friday, leaving 12 dead and causing millions of dollars' worth of damage. Beach towns were submerged, power supplies to nearly one million homes were lost, and severe flooding was reported in low-lying areas.

The hurricane hit shore near Cape Fear, North Carolina, late Thursday with 115 mph winds. Most of the people killed were motorists whose cars were hit by falling trees. On Friday Fran moved to Virginia and was downgraded to a tropical storm. President Clinton has declared North Carolina a major disaster area, opening the way for federal assistance.

S	M	T	W	T	F	S
1	2	3	4	5	6	7
8	9	10	11	12	13	14
15	16	17	18	19	20	21
22	23	24	25	26	27	28
29	30					

New York, 8
Pete Sampras and Steffi Graf win the singles titles at the US Open tennis championships at Flushing Meadow.

New York, 10
The UN General Assembly endorses the Comprehesive Test Ban Treaty, a universal ban on nuclear testing. (→ September 24)

Fort Worth, TX, 10
The murder of 16-year-old Adrianne Jones is blamed on two outstanding 18-year-old students at top military academies—boyfriend and girlfriend David Graham and Diane Zamora.

Washington, DC, 10
The Senate approves the Defense of Marriage Act, a bill that would deny federal recognition of gay marriages.

Puerto Rico, 12
After killing 15 people in Puerto Rico, Hurricane Hortense bypasses the Bahamas and heads toward the coast of New England.

Burbank, CA, 12
Actress Sondra Locke sues former companion Clint Eastwood for more than $2 million, claiming that the star sabotaged her career. (→ September 24)

Jamestown, VA, 12
Archeologists discover the remains of the first permanent English settlement in America, the 1607 Jamestown fort, along with the grave of an early settler.

Volusia County, FL, 13
County Councillor Lynne Plaskett attracts national attention when she says on TV that aliens cured her of cancer.

Washington, DC, 13
The White House refuses to release Bill Clinton's health records, admitting that they contain details that might "compromise his dignity."

Montreal, 14
The US wins the World Cup of Hockey in a dramatic finish, coming from behind to beat Canada 5-2.

Deaths
September 9. Bill Monroe, father of Bluegrass music, at age 84.

September 10. Joanne Dru, actress who made 40 films, many of them Westerns, in Beverly Hills, at age 73.

PIAN DEL RE, ITALY, FRIDAY 13
Italian separatist calls for new state of Padania

The Italian separatist leader of the Northern League, Umberto Bossi, today launched a crusade on the banks of the Po River as a prelude to the declaration of independence for his self-styled northern republic. After symbolically filling a flask with water from the source of the Po at Pian del Re, he instigated a "March to the Sea," which would culminate in Venice with the proclamation of Padanian independence.

After gaining 10.6 percent of the vote in the last general election, the Northern League has gained support in northern Italy based on dissatisfaction with high taxes, government bureaucracy, and perceived southern inefficiency and crime.

Italian supporters of the Northern League proclaim an "independent" Padania.

LOS ANGELES, MONDAY 9
Gulliver and Frasier top Emmys

The eponymous hero of Frasier, *Kelsey Grammer (left), with his on-screen father.*

Ted Danson in Gulliver's Travels.

Tonight's ceremony marked the fiftieth anniversary of the TV industry's Emmy awards. Top winners, with five Emmys each, were *Gulliver's Travels*, which stars Ted Danson, and the cult psychic-investigation hit, the *X-Files*. The most-nominated series, *ER*, won only one out of a possible 17 awards, although this was the prestigious best drama award. *Frasier* won four Emmys, including its third successive award for best comedy.

NYPD Blue's Dennis Franz won the best actor award for the second time, and, after two previous nominations, British actress Helen Mirren took her first Emmy for her role as detective Jane Tennison in *Prime Suspect*.

IRAQ, MONDAY 9
Kurds backed by Iraq triumph over rivals

Kurdish forces supported by President Saddam Hussein's Iraqi government today attacked and routed a rival Kurdish faction. Troops of the Kurdish Democratic Party (KDP) stormed toward the Iranian border, throwing back forces of the Patriotic Union of Kurdistan (PUK) in disarray. KDP forces have also captured the PUK stronghold of Sulaymaniyah. Many Kurds have fled their homes, fearful of the Iraqi involvement in the KDP advance. (→ October 14)

Rome, Sunday 8. Naturalized black Italian Denny Mendez has caused uproar by being voted Miss Italy. There are complaints that the former Dominican does not reflect "Italian beauty."

LITTLE ROCK, TUESDAY 10

Former Clinton associate won't testify

Wearing handcuffs, Susan McDougal is led away from court to begin her sentence.

In one of the stranger twists in the Whitewater affair, Susan McDougal, a former business partner of President Bill Clinton, has gone to jail rather than testify before a grand jury about the president's role in the Whitewater case. She was being asked to say whether Clinton had helped her obtain an illegal loan.

McDougal has surprised observers by her decision not to testify. She could have taken the stand and simply stated the truth of President Clinton's account or alternatively denied knowledge of proceedings, thus avoiding the contempt charges.

Yesterday, McDougal was taken to a county jail in Conway, Arkansas, with cuffed hands and manacled feet, facing the possibility of an 18-month sentence for contempt of court. There are already suggestions, however, that she may benefit from a presidential pardon after the November election.

McDougal claims in her defense that the Whitewater special prosecutor, Republican Kenneth Starr, is guilty of partisanship, but this allegation is not thought to carry much legal weight.

Venice, Sunday 8. Liam Neeson wins the best actor award at the Venice Film Festival for his performance in the lead role of *Michael Collins*, which also won the best film award.

NEW YORK, WEDNESDAY 11

Sheryl Crow banned by Wal-Mart

Singer Sheryl Crow, locked in battle with chain-store Wal-Mart over song lyrics.

The US discount retail chain Wal-Mart today refused to stock Sheryl Crow's new album because it contains song lyrics about the store's gun sales. The song "Love is a Good Thing" implies that children can buy guns at Wal-Mart, which they subsequently use to kill each other.

Wal-Mart spokesman Dale Ingram said that it was "unfair and irresponsible" to suggest that "we contribute to the harm of children." Ingram said that the stores only sold weapons by catalog, and not to children. The ban could lose Sheryl Crow up to 400,000 album sales.

ZURICH, SATURDAY 14

Stolen Jewish gold held by Swiss banks

Stung by the revelation that Swiss financial institutions have held on to gold stolen from Jews and deposited in bank vaults by the Nazis, the Swiss government has decided to publish a decree next Monday that orders all bank records to be handed over to a special investigating committee.

How much gold is actually in the vaults is disputed, but Jewish groups claim that as much as $6 billion at today's prices is still unaccounted for. Swiss sources say that there is only $30 million in the dormant accounts, but, whatever the final figure, the problem remains of finding the rightful owners. At present 700 people are making claims for the money, but one of the lawyers representing the claimants believes that much of the money has been spirited out of the accounts since 1945. (→ October 22)

RIO DE JANEIRO, THURSDAY 12

Amazon rain forest continues to shrink

Despite claims by the Brazilian government that strict environmental laws have slowed the destruction of the Amazonian rain forests, recent figures suggest that forest clearing is on the increase: deforestation rose by 34 percent during 1990 to 1994. Brazil has announced measures to crack down on illegal logging, but environmentalists argue that this is merely window dressing to counter hostile world opinion.

Vanishing asset: Brazilian loggers cut a swathe through the Amazonian forest.

September

S	M	T	W	T	F	S
1	2	3	4	5	6	7
8	9	10	11	12	13	14
15	16	17	18	19	20	21
22	23	24	25	26	27	28
29	30					

Monaco, 16
Princess Stephanie of Monaco files for divorce from her husband, Daniel Ducret, following the publication of pictures of him with a stripper.

New York, 16
Ellen DeGeneres, star of ABC's *Ellen*, is said by her agent to be considering whether her character in the show should "come out" as gay.

Washington, DC, 16
The Pentagon reveals that US military commanders ignored terrorist threats on the apartment complex in Saudi Arabia that was bombed last June, killing 19.

Santa Monica, CA, 17
The civil suit against O. J. Simpson, brought by the parents of Nicole Brown Simpson and Ron Goldman, opens. O. J. Simpson will be forced to testify during the trial. (→ October 23)

South Korea, 19
Troops shoot seven North Koreans on the second day of a manhunt for infiltrators who came ashore from a submarine. Six more infiltrators are thought to be at large. (→ September 25)

Chico, CA, 19
Presidential candidate Bob Dole falls 4 ft from a stage during a campaign address. (→ October 6)

Space station Mir, 19
The space shuttle Atlantis docks with the Russian space station Mir to take astronaut Shannon Lucid back to Earth after her record-breaking six months in orbit. (→ September 26)

Moscow, 20
President Boris Yeltsin's doctors publicly express concern about the president's ability to withstand major heart surgery. (→ November 5)

Deaths
September 14. Juliet Prowse, dancer and actress, of cancer in Los Angeles, at age 59.

September 16. Politician McGeorge Bundy, a former key advisor to Presidents Kennedy and Johnson, in Boston, at age 77.

September 20. Hungarian Paul Erdos, one of the century's greatest mathematicians, in Warsaw, at age 83.

US, Friday 20. *First Wives Club* opens across the US today, and may open a new round in the battle of the sexes. Diane Keaton, Goldie Hawn, and Bette Midler play college classmates who band together to seek revenge after their wealthy husbands desert them.

MOSCOW, THURSDAY 19
Prime minister will step in for Yeltsin

President Boris Yeltsin last night signed a decree that will hand over all power to the prime minister, Viktor Chernomyrdin, while Yeltsin undergoes heart surgery. The move ends a week of debate over who will control the nuclear button while the president is being operated upon.

The issue of who will substitute for the president has become pressing because of suspicions that Yeltsin is more ill than admitted. He has been out of public life and under medical care almost constantly since his reelection in July. A date is still to be set for his operation. (→ September 20)

AUSTRALIA, SATURDAY 21
Ancient art find confounds theories

Researchers are claiming to have found rock carvings 76,000 years old and 176,000-year-old stone tools in Australia. If correctly dated, the finds undermine current theories about primitive man. Modern *Homo sapiens* was not thought to have reached Australia until 60,000 years ago. This suggests the art and tools were the work of a predecessor, *Homo erectus*, previously thought too unintelligent to have navigated to the antipodes.

Maryland, Tuesday 17. Former US Vice President Spiro Agnew, who resigned from office in 1973, dies of leukemia at age 77.

IRVING, TX, TUESDAY 17
Thousands sworn in as US citizens

People from 113 different countries take the oath of allegiance at Texas Stadium.

Ten thousand new US citizens were sworn in today at a mass naturalization ceremony at Texas Stadium in Irving. It is to be followed by an even bigger event in San Jose, California, tomorrow. These mass swearing-ins are part of a surge in naturalization, the biggest in US history. Experts say the trend is due to anti-immigration laws and public sentiment, but there have also been accusations that the Clinton administration is trying to turn out new Democratic voters on a large scale before the election.

BOSNIA, WEDNESDAY 18

Hardliners hold sway in Bosnia elections

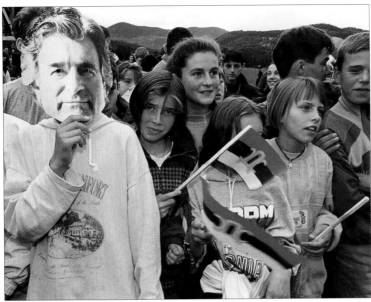

A Serb wears a mask of Radovan Karadzic, showing support for a wanted war criminal.

Muslim supporters of Alija Izetbegovic attend an election rally at Tuzla.

The good news from Bosnia is that elections have taken place without violence. The bad news is that the voters in all three of Bosnia's ethnic groups have backed hardliners who are likely to reinforce the divisions that threaten to tear Bosnia apart.

Under the terms of the Dayton accords that ended the Bosnian civil war last year, Bosnia is to be run by a tripartite presidency, with one representative elected by each ethnic group. The Muslims have elected Alija Izetbegovic, the man who led them through the civil war. He will chair the presidency. Bosnian Serbs voted for Momcilo Krajisnik, a committed separatist, who is under investigation by the War Crimes Tribunal for his part in ethnic cleansing during the civil war. Croats elected Kresimir Zubak, who is said to favor Croatia taking over Croat areas of Bosnia.

It is difficult to imagine these three men working together for peace and harmony. US diplomat Richard Holbrooke, architect of the Dayton accords, said he is just anxious to see the new presidential institutions functioning. (→ September 23)

SOUTH KOREA, WED. 18

Submarine off coast raises alarm

South Korean troops are hunting for infiltrators from North Korea, after an abandoned submarine was found off South Korea's east coast, near the town of Kangung. The bodies of 11 infiltrators were found in nearby mountains. They had apparently shot themselves to avoid being captured. One soldier was caught alive and has reportedly told his interrogators that 13 other North Korean soldiers are still at large.

Infiltrations are of serious concern to South Korea. Military analysts have warned that a Northern invasion would be preceded by the arrival of saboteurs. (→ September 19)

The abandoned North Korean submarine.

SOUTH AFRICA, WED. 18

De Klerk accused by hitman

A former police colonel convicted of being an assassin during the apartheid era has said that F.W. de Klerk, leader of the opposition party in South Africa, knew of covert operations that existed while he was president.

Eugene de Kock headed a secret death squad in the 1980s and early 1990s, and was last month convicted of six murders. During his plea for leniency today, he told the court that de Klerk ordered an attack on a home in Transkei in 1993, where five people were killed. De Klerk last month denied knowledge of any atrocities before the Truth and Reconciliation Commission. (→ September 26)

LAS VEGAS, MONDAY 16

Rap under fire after star's death

Slain rapper Tupac Shakur.

The death by shooting of rapper Tupac Shakur is raising questions once again about the influence of rap music. Shakur, 25, was shot four times in the chest on his way to a nightclub on Saturday 6. He died the following Friday. Shakur is being mourned in his community as a black victim of an uncaring society, but others see him as a rapper who fittingly died by the violent culture glorified in his lyrics.

Washington, DC, Sunday 15. Bill Clinton awards the Presidential Medal of Freedom to 83-year-old Rosa Parks, the woman who sparked the modern civil rights movement 41 years ago when she refused to give up her bus seat to a white passenger in Alabama.

S	M	T	W	T	F	S
1	2	3	4	5	6	7
8	9	10	11	12	13	14
15	16	17	18	19	20	21
22	23	24	25	26	27	28
29	30					

Atlanta, 22
The FBI accepts that there is no solid evidence linking former security guard Richard Jewell to the bombing at the Atlanta Olympics. (→ October 28)

Chepstow, Wales, 22
The US women's golf team defeats Europe 17-11 to win the Solheim Cup.

Bosnia, 23
European observers monitoring last week's Bosnian elections say they cannot be called "free" or "fair," but that the level of fraud does not invalidate the results.

Media, PA, 24
Millionaire John du Pont, accused in connection with the killing of wrestler Dave Schultz, is declared incompetent to stand trial and sent to a mental hospital.

Hollywood, 25
It is announced that John Travolta is to play Bill Clinton in the film version of the political satire *Primary Colors*.

Alexandria, VA, 25
Robert Kim, a US citizen of Korean origin, has been arrested by the FBI on charges of spying for South Korea.

Johannesburg, South Africa, 26
Eugene de Kock, head of a South African police hit squad in the apartheid era, claims that a South African intelligence agent killed Swedish prime minister Olaf Palme in 1986.

San Jose, CA, 26
Richard Davis, convicted of the killing of 12-year-old Polly Klaas in 1993, is sentenced to death.

Washington, DC, 26
The Transportation Department authorizes Valujet Airlines to resume flights. Valujet was grounded in June, in the wake of the Everglades jet crash.

Cape Canaveral, FL, 26
Astronaut Shannon Lucid arrives back on Earth after 188 days and five hours in space. She traveled 75 million miles during the longest space voyage for a woman and an American.

Hobart, Tasmania, 30
Martin Bryant pleads not guilty to the Port Arthur massacre last April in which 35 people died.

Deaths
September 29. Shusaku Endo, Japanese novelist, at age 73.

NEW YORK, TUESDAY 24
Global test ban treaty signed

At the United Nations in New York today, the five acknowledged nuclear powers—the United States, Russia, France, Britain, and China—signed a Comprehensive Test Ban Treaty that officially bans all nuclear explosions.

President Bill Clinton signed with the pen that President John F. Kennedy used 33 years ago to sign the first partial nuclear test ban. In a speech to the UN General Assembly, Clinton said the treaty was "the longest sought, hardest fought prize in arms control history."

However, India, which carried out a nuclear test in 1974, has refused to sign the treaty unless the major powers agree to abolish their nuclear arsenals.

DARWIN, WEDNESDAY 25
Patient exercises "right to die"

A terminally ill cancer patient in Australia's Northern Territory has become the first man to end his own life legally under the Territory's 1995 voluntary euthanasia legislation. The patient, who has not been named, used a computer program called Deliverance to activate a lethal injection. The euthanasia law is being challenged in Australia's High Court.

Burbank, CA, Tuesday 24. Actor Clint Eastwood has had to pay up after being sued by former partner Sondra Locke. She claimed he tricked her into dropping a palimony suit by offering a phony film deal.

Washington, DC, Tuesday 24. The first lady breakfasts with Princess Diana at the White House. The visit was a welcome distraction for Hillary Clinton from further allegations linking her to fraudulent deals at the Madison Guaranty Savings and Loan.

KABUL, AFGHANISTAN, FRIDAY 27
Taleban Islamic fighters take Kabul

A Taleban guerrilla presents a smiling image after the Muslim fighters' takeover of Kabul.

In a dramatic turn to Afghanistan's seemingly endless civil war, forces of the Islamic fundamentalist Taleban group today took control of the Afghan capital, Kabul.

Afghanistan has been the scene of chaotic fighting between rival guerrilla groups ever since the communist president, Muhammad Najibullah, was deposed in 1992. One of the Taleban's first acts on entering Kabul was to seize Najibullah from a UN compound and shoot him dead. Najibullah's body was then hanged outside the presidential palace.

The Afghan government's defense chief, Ahmed Shah Massoud, has fled from Kabul. He will continue fighting the Taleban from his power base to the north of the city. (→ October 4)

JERUSALEM, FRIDAY 27

Seventy killed in West Bank clashes

Israeli security forces walk past the Dome of the Rock, one of the Muslim holy places in Jerusalem at the heart of the current conflict.

A dispute that focuses on the Muslim holy places in Jerusalem has precipitated the worst clashes between Israel and the Palestinians since the peace process began in 1993. Three days of clashes in Jerusalem and towns on the West Bank have left at least 70 people dead.

Palestinians rioted in protest at Israel's decision to open a new entrance to a tunnel near Al-Aqsa mosque in Jerusalem's Old City. The mosque, near the Dome of the Rock, is the third holiest place in Islam.

When Israeli security forces penetrated Palestinian-controlled areas on the West Bank in pursuit of stone-throwing rioters, Palestinian security forces exchanged fire with Israeli soldiers. Today three people were killed in clashes at Al-Aqsa mosque itself. Israel is threatening to send tanks into the West Bank to quell the uprising. (→ October 2)

A wounded Palestinian is carried to safety in the West Bank town of Ramallah.

Lexington, NC, Wednesday 25. Six-year-old Johnathan Prevette (seen here, bottom left, with his family) has been punished by his school for kissing a female classmate on the cheek. The kiss has been defined by the school as sexual harassment.

LONDON, TUESDAY 24

IRA man shot dead in London

The British police force are claiming a major victory over IRA terrorism after a series of raids yesterday at sites in and around London.

The police raids left one suspected terrorist dead and five more under arrest. The dead man was named as Diarmuid O'Neill. He was shot when police raided a guesthouse in west London. He appears to have been unarmed.

The police also seized a large cache of arms and more than ten tons of homemade explosives. (→ October 7)

Blood stains the path of the house where IRA man Diarmuid O'Neill was shot.

October

Lima, Peru, 2
A Peruvian airliner crashes into the Pacific Ocean a half hour after taking off from Lima. All 70 people on board are feared dead.

Washington, DC, 2
The Supreme Court agrees to consider whether terminally ill patients have a right to assisted suicide. A ruling is expected by July 1997.

Washington, DC, 2
The Pentagon announces that 5,000 US troops are to start moving into Bosnia to cover the withdrawal of the NATO-led peace force in December. The 5,000 troops are scheduled to stay in Bosnia until March 1997.

Los Angeles, 3
Former detective Mark Fuhrman pleads no contest to a charge of perjury arising from his false testimony in last year's O.J. Simpson trial. Fuhrman is given probation and a $200 fine. (→ October 8)

Washington, DC, 3
President Clinton signs a proclamation banning Burmese leaders or their family members from entering the US. The measure is a response to the detention of Burmese pro-democracy activists.

San Francisco, 3
State attorney general Dan Lungren calls on newspapers to pull Garry Trudeau's *Doonesbury* cartoon, which is critical of the state's raid on the San Francisco Cannabis Buyers Club last August. The club claims it supplies cannabis only for doctor-approved uses.

Moscow, 4
Russian president Boris Yeltsin dismisses six senior generals, including General Yevgeni Podkolzin, commander of the elite paratroops. (→ October 16)

New York, 5
Wayne Gretzky and Mark Messier make their debuts for the New York Rangers against the Boston Bruins at the start of the ice hockey season.

Deaths
October 2. Robert Bourassa, former prime minister of Quebec, at age 63.

October 5. Seymour Cray, computer designer, at age 71.

Middle East summit fails to heal the fresh wounds

The White House summit: Left to right, Arafat, Hussein, Clinton, and Netanyahu.

President Bill Clinton's latest attempt at the role of international peacemaker ended in partial failure today when a hastily organized Middle East peace summit ended without agreement on crucial issues.

The emergency talks, held over two days at the White House, brought the Palestinian leader Yasir Arafat and Israeli prime minister, Benjamin Netanyahu, face to face for the first time since last week's violence in Jerusalem and the West Bank plunged Israel into crisis. President Clinton chaired the meeting. King Hussein of Jordan was also present.

The Israelis and Palestinians agreed to resume talks on the withdrawal of Israeli troops from the West Bank city of Hebron, but reached no agreement on the issues behind the recent violence. (→ October 23)

WASHINGTON, DC, TUES. 1

Soros pledges $50 million for immigrants

George Soros, billionaire financier and philanthropist, has pledged $50 million to aid legal immigrants who he believes will suffer as a result of recent welfare reforms.

Soros said: "The Statue of Liberty embraces those 'yearning to breathe free,' but the current mean-spirited attack on immigrants threatens to choke them." Born in Hungary, Soros is himself an immigrant.

Chicago, Saturday 5. As the presidential election approaches, campaigners from both the pro-gun and anti-gun lobbies have taken to the streets to publicize their views.

VATNAJOKULL, ICELAND, FRIDAY 4

Volcano threatens Iceland

Gas and ash spews out from the volcano underneath Europe's largest glacier.

A volcano is in eruption underneath the largest ice sheet in Europe. It threatens to cause severe floods that could devastate large areas of Iceland.

Bardhabunga volcano is 130 miles east of Iceland's capital, Reykjavik. It lies beneath the Vatnajokull glacier, which covers almost one tenth of the surface of Iceland. Black clouds of ash and gas are spewing out through a fissure in the ice sheet. Experts fear that much of the glacier will melt, raising water levels to catastrophic heights. (→ November 5)

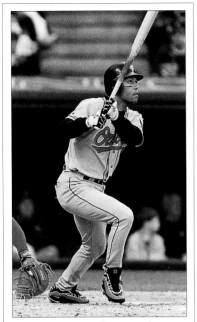

Cleveland, Saturday 5. Roberto Alomar hits a homer to take Baltimore Orioles into the AL Championship series. Last week Alomar came close to causing an umpires' boycott of the play-offs by spitting on umpire John Hirschbeck. (→ October 10)

Many mammals face extinction

More than 1,000 mammal species are at risk of extinction, including one third of all primates, humankind's closest animal relatives.

These figures are from the latest Red List of endangered species issued by the IUCN-World Conservation Union. The organization has been monitoring animal survival for 35 years. It now believes that previous Red Lists may have understated the risk to many species.

The major threat to most species is the destruction or pollution of their natural habitats. US interior secretary Bruce Babbitt said the report clearly shows that "unless people of all nations make extraordinary efforts, we face a looming natural catastrophe of almost biblical proportions."

Stockholm, Thursday 3. Polish poet Wislawa Szymborska has been awarded the 1996 Nobel Prize for Literature. The citation praised Szymborska, age 73, for her "ironic precision." Poland's former president, Lech Walesa, described her as "great of heart and pen."

Nerve gas hit 15,000 US soldiers

A Pentagon spokesman has admitted today that more than 15,000 US soldiers may have been exposed to nerve or mustard gas during the Gulf War in 1991. The Pentagon first said last year that some Americans might have suffered exposure to chemical weapons, but only 1,100 men were then said to be involved.

The risk of exposure occurred when US troops blew up arms dumps at Khamisiya in southern Iraq. It may be linked to the symptoms known as Gulf War syndrome.

US soldiers during the 1991 Gulf War.

KABUL, AFGHANISTAN, FRIDAY 4

Taleban drives women under cover

Only very young women, classified as children, are allowed to show their faces in Taleban-ruled Kabul.

After last week's takeover by Taleban guerrillas, the people of Kabul are enjoying a rare interlude of peace. But they are also having to adapt to a rigorous Islamic regime that intends to control every detail of daily life. All government employees have been ordered to grow beards. Television has been banned and music cassettes are being confiscated.

All women except the very young have been ordered to wear a full veil in public. Women have reportedly been beaten with sticks by Taleban fighters for minor infringements of the new dress code, such as showing a few inches of ankle. Women have also been banned from working, a potentially fatal regulation for the many widows who have no other source of income or support. (→ October 10)

October

Copenhagen, Denmark, 6
A feud between rival gangs of bikers in Scandinavia reaches a new pitch of violence as an anti-tank missile is fired.

Bordeaux, France, 6
A bomb destroys the Bordeaux office of French prime minister Alain Juppé.

Rome, 8
The Pope has his appendix removed in a 50-minute operation. Doctors say there are no complications.

New York, 8
Former Los Angeles police officer Mark Fuhrman, interviewed by Diane Sawyer on ABC's *Prime Time Live,* apologizes for using racist language, but denies planting evidence in the O.J. Simpson case. (→ October 23)

Glen Canyon, AZ, 9
The artificial flood created in March to renew the ecology of the Colorado River is declared a success. Studies by more than 100 scientists reveal that fish, vegetation, and some endangered species benefited from the flood.

Mexico City, 10
Mexican police say they have found a human skull buried on the ranch of Raul Salinas, brother of former Mexican president Carlos Salinas. Prosecutors are trying to link Raul Salinas to the political assassination of Jose Ruiz Massieu in 1994.

New York, 11
Researchers from the City University of New York claim that women who have undergone an abortion have a 30 percent higher risk of contracting breast cancer.

Berlin, 11
The German authorities announce that they have arrested two people, a Palestinian man and a German woman, in connection with the 1986 Berlin nightclub bombing in which two US servicemen were killed.

New York, 12
Some senior federal air-safety officials say that the most probable cause of the TWA 800 airliner crash is mechanical failure. (→ October 22)

Deaths
October 12. René Lacoste, French tennis star and sportswear entrepreneur, at age 92.

NEW YORK, THURSDAY 10

Yankees fan lends a hand

Jeff Maier, a 12-year-old baseball fan from New Jersey, helped the New York Yankees to a precious narrow victory in the opening game of the AL Championship series last night.

The Yankees were trailing the Baltimore Orioles 4–3 when Maier leaned down over the right-field wall to flip a drive hit by Yankees' Derek Jeter into the stands. Baltimore right fielder Tony Tarasco had seemed poised to catch the ball and the batter should probably have been given out. But umpire Rich Garcia did not see Maier's intervention, and a home run was called over strident Baltimore protests. The Yankees' Bernie Williams followed up with another homer, and his team ran out winners 5–4.

With the Yankees playing in the AL Championship series for the first time in 15 years and baseball mania seizing New York, Maier has become an instant celebrity. He described the event as "pretty cool." (→ October 17)

HARTFORD, CT, SUNDAY 6

First TV debate leaves polls unchanged

Sticking to issues: The first Clinton-Dole duel was devoid of dramatic flourishes or gaffes.

Republican presidential challenger Bob Dole, trailing in the opinion polls, is looking to his two planned televised debates with President Bill Clinton to swing the public mood radically in his favor.

But the first debate, broadcast from Bushnell Auditorium in Hartford, Connecticut, this evening, suggested he would fail to make a dramatic impact. About 70 million viewers tuned in, the largest sign of interest so far in a campaign that has been dismissed by many as lackluster. Few are likely to have changed their minds as the candidates worked over familiar themes in a civilized way, avoiding personal attacks. (→ October 16)

Washington, DC, Saturday 12. An AIDS Memorial Quilt was laid along Washington's Mall this weekend in memory of those killed by the disease. Each square of the mile-long quilt represents one of America's 350,000 AIDS victims. Actress Elizabeth Taylor later led a candlelight remembrance march.

DURBAN, FRIDAY 11
Acquittal for apartheid general

General Malan (left) after the verdict.

Many black South Africans were shocked as General Magnus Malan, a former defense minister of the apartheid era, walked free from court today. Malan and nine others had been accused of authorizing death squads, including one that massacred 13 people in a township in 1987.

Nelson Mandela, the South African president, refused to condemn the not-guilty verdicts. He said: "The judicial findings must be respected, even, or especially, by those who are aggrieved by the result."

STOCKHOLM, FRIDAY 11
Nobel Prize for Timor campaigners

Peace Prize winner Jose Ramos-Horta.

The Nobel Peace Prize was awarded today to two campaigners for the independence of East Timor, a former Portuguese colony ruled by Indonesia since 1976. One of the laureates, Jose Ramos-Horta, is leader of Fretilin, the East Timorese resistance movement. The other is Carlos Belli, the Bishop of Dili, the East Timorese capital. An Indonesian minister expressed anger at the award to "political adventurist" Ramos-Horta. (→ October 15)

LISBURN, NORTHERN IRELAND, MONDAY 7
Terrorists bomb army base

Two car bombs exploded inside the Northern Ireland headquarters of the British Army today, injuring more than 30 people. At least one victim is not expected to survive.

Thiepval Barracks, Lisburn, is probably the most heavily defended place in Northern Ireland. Somehow the terrorists were able to penetrate the tight security with two explosive-laden vehicles. The first went off in a parking lot just inside the entrance to the base. The second detonated near the base's medical center ten minutes later. It was presumably intended to hit casualties being carried for treatment after the first explosion.

No organization has yet said that it carried out the terrorist attack. It is thought to be the work of the IRA or of another breakaway Republican group. The British prime minister, John Major, described the bombings as "wicked beyond belief."

AFGHANISTAN, THURSDAY 10
New military alliance drives back Taleban fighters

Taleban fighters prepare to resist the counter-attack on Kabul from the north.

When the Taleban occupied Kabul, Afghanistan, last month, it seemed a turning point in the country's relentless warfare. But the Taleban have only succeeded in uniting their foes.

In the small town of Khinjan, 100 miles north of Kabul, faction leaders Ahmed Shah Massoud, Abdul Rashid Dustam, and Abdul Karim Kalilli today forged a formidable alliance. Between them, these men already control one third of Afghanistan. Now their forces are driving the Taleban back toward Kabul. Still, no force is strong enough to win a victory and impose peace. (→ October 27)

New York, Thursday 10. More than 300 firefighters tackled a blaze today at the GE building, site of the NBC headquarters. Eleven people were injured and local TV programs were affected.

OAKLAND, MI, MONDAY 7
Talk show murder trial opens

At Oakland Circuit Court today, Jonathan Schmitz is on trial for the murder of his gay admirer, Scott Amedure. But many people feel the real accused in the case is a TV talk show hosted by Jenny Jones.

Last March, Schmitz was invited on to the show to meet someone who had a crush on him. The mystery admirer was revealed to be Amedure. Schmitz, a heterosexual, claims to have been humiliated by the trick played on him. Three days later, he allegedly shot Amedure dead. (→ November 13)

New York, Friday 11. William Vickrey, a Canadian-born economist, died today—only two days after sharing the Nobel Prize for Economics. Vickrey taught for many years at Columbia University.

S	M	T	W	T	F	S
		1	2	3	4	5
6	7	8	9	10	11	12
13	14	15	16	17	18	19
20	21	22	23	24	25	26
27	28	29	30	31		

Washington, DC, 14
Reports emerge that contributions have been made to President Bill Clinton's election campaign by wealthy Indonesians and may be linked to US trade-policy favors for Indonesia. (→ October 29)

Iraq, 14
Kurdish forces hostile to President Saddam Hussein's Iraqi government recover most of the ground lost in last month's fighting in northern Iraq.

East Timor, 15
Indonesian president Suharto visits East Timor but makes it clear he will make no concessions in the wake of the Nobel Peace Prize awards to two East Timor activists.

London, 16
The British government says it will outlaw private ownership of almost all handguns. The move is a response to the public outcry over the massacre of 16 school children and a teacher in Dunblane, Scotland, in March.

Atlanta, 17
The Atlanta Braves defeat the St. Louis Cardinals to win the NL Championship and qualify for the World Series against the Yankees. (→ October 19)

Guatemala City, 17
At least 78 people are crushed to death at a World Cup soccer match.

New York, 18
Scientists announce they have found an "absolute" link between smoking and lung cancer, proving what statistical studies have long suggested.

New York, 19
A Delta Airlines plane landing at La Guardia airport nearly crashes when its landing gear collapses.

New York, 19
The first match of the World Series between the Atlanta Braves and the New York Yankees is rained out. (→ October 26)

Deaths
October 15. Pierre Franey, renowned chef, *New York Times* food writer, and cookbook author, in Southampton, England, at age 75.

SAN DIEGO, CA, WEDNESDAY 16
Candidates upstaged by race for Congress

In the final TV presidential debate in San Diego this evening, Bob Dole pulled no punches in attacking Bill Clinton's moral character. But the Republican challenger shows no signs of denting Clinton's lead in the polls.

With Dole's chances of winning increasingly forlorn, public attention is turning to the battle for control of Congress. Some individual contests are being bitterly fought, such as that between Democrat Robert Toricelli and Republican Dick Zimmer in New Jersey, Democrat John Kerry's tussle with Governor William Weld in Massachusetts, and Harvey Gantt's rematch with Jesse Helms in North Carolina. (→ November 6)

Senator Strom Thurmond from South Carolina is standing for reelection at age 93.

London, Tuesday 15. Rolling Stone Mick Jagger and his wife, Texan model Jerry Hall, are said to be splitting up. Hall saw a divorce lawyer after articles appeared in the press linking Jagger with a Czech model.

NEW YORK, MONDAY 14
Wall Street bull run drives on

The Dow Jones industrial average today topped 6,000 points for the first time ever, closing at 6,010. Six years ago, in October 1990, the index slumped to 2,365. Since then the bull market on Wall Street has surged continuously, giving investors an average growth in their capital of over 150 percent.

No bull market in the history of Wall Street has ever lasted so long, and only one has been larger in percentage terms—the surge that ended in disaster in the crash of 1929.

TOKYO, SATURDAY 19
Japanese election balanced between past and future

Japanese voters go to the polls tomorrow for a general election that will decide whether the country embraces social and economic reform.

Conservatives and traditionalists will vote for the Liberal Democratic Party, which has dominated Japan for over 40 years. The current prime minister, Ryutaro Hashimoto, hopes to be confirmed in office by a solid victory for the LDP.

A range of other parties, including the New Frontier Party and the recently formed Democratic Party, are advocating major changes to open up Japanese society and cut back the entrenched bureaucracy. Most foreign observers consider such changes long overdue. (→ October 20)

The Democratic Party, a newcomer in Japanese politics, campaigns in the general election.

BELGIUM, SATURDAY 19
Popular protests mount over pedophile scandal

The Marc Dutroux case, involving the abduction, sexual abuse, and murder of an unknown number of young girls, this week swelled into a massive crisis of confidence in the Belgian political and legal system.

Public outrage peaked on Monday when Jean-Marc Connerotte, the magistrate who first uncovered the pedophile ring, was taken off the case for accepting a meal from campaigners against child abuse. This was said to compromise his impartiality.

Connerotte's removal from the case led to a wave of protests, including strikes by transport workers. Many Belgians fear a cover-up by senior politicians somehow linked to the scandal. A mass demonstration is to be held in Brussels on Sunday.

Belgians gather to mourn lost children and protest the mishandling of the investigation.

Miami, Sunday 13. Pressure mounts on Jimmy Johnson, coach of the Miami Dolphins, as he struggles to give his team the success that was expected when he was hired in January.

WASHINGTON, DC, MON. 14
Crime in US falling, says FBI

According to the FBI's Uniform Crime Report, crime in the US is at its lowest level for ten years. Violent crime in 1995 was 4 percent down on the previous year, and murders fell by as much as 8 percent.

A statement from the White House claimed that the improved figures proved the Clinton administration's anticrime strategy was working.

Los Angeles, Tuesday 15. Pop star Madonna, seen here in her latest movie role as Evita, gave birth yesterday to a girl, named Lourdes Maria Ciccione Leon. The baby's father is Carlos Leon, a Cuban-born fitness instructor.

MOSCOW, WEDNESDAY 16
Yeltsin fires Lebed in dramatic television coup

The Russian president, Boris Yeltsin, tonight publicly fired his security chief, General Alexander Lebed, the most popular politician in Russia.

Yeltsin interrupted the evening's scheduled television broadcasts to address the Russian people from the sanatorium where he is awaiting a heart operation. He accused Lebed of using his position to run a disguised campaign for the presidency. "I can no longer tolerate this situation," Yeltsin said, "and I am forced to relieve General Lebed of his position as secretary of the security council." He then dramatically signed the general's dismissal decree in front of the television cameras.

Lebed responded to the dismissal with a contemptuous insouciance. He said he was "not bothered in the slightest," and that he had "long since stopped being offended." But he warned that he was the only person trusted in Chechnya—"and not only in Chechnya," he added.

Lebed secured Yeltsin's reelection when he threw his support behind the Russian leader in the second round of the presidential ballot. But Lebed soon emerged as a potential rival. Tonight he vowed he would not contest the presidency "while Russia has a living president." The future of Russia now depends on the outcome of Yeltsin's operation. (→ November 5)

Russia's most popular politician: General Alexander Lebed, with his wife Inna.

S	M	T	W	T	F	S
		1	2	3	4	5
6	7	8	9	10	11	12
13	14	15	16	17	18	19
20	21	22	23	24	25	26
27	28	29	30	31		

Tokyo, 20
The general election in Japan fails to produce a clear majority for the ruling Liberal Democratic party. Prime Minister Ryutaro Hashimoto remains in power, but his party will have to build a coalition.

Foxboro, MA, 20
In the first Major League Soccer championship, DC United come from behind to beat Los Angeles Galaxy 3-2 in overtime.

Eastern Zaire, 21
The UN reports that 220,000 Hutu refugees have left their camps and are fleeing into the hills in order to escape the conflict between the Zairian military and Tutsi guerrillas. (→ October 31)

New York, 22
A lawyer representing 25 families of TWA Flight 800 crash victims files lawsuits against Boeing and TWA, claiming that a mechanical fault caused the crash. (→ November 8)

Zurich, 22
Switzerland admits that assets of Polish Holocaust victims were used to compensate Swiss nationals for property lost to communist Poland.

Tokyo, 22
Copper trader Yasuo Hamanaka, who was accused last June by his former employers Sumitomo Corp. of causing $2.6 billion in losses through unauthorized trading, is arrested on charges of forgery.

Florida, 23
Lawyer F. Lee Bailey is suing the federal government for $10 million. He asserts that money the court seized from him earlier this year, on the grounds that it came from a drug trafficker, rightfully belongs to him.

Dallas, 24
Republican presidential candidate Bob Dole sends his campaign manager to Dallas to ask Ross Perot to withdraw from the race and endorse Dole. Perot declines, calling the request "weird and totally inconsequential."

New York, 25
New research suggests that simple life forms may have appeared on earth 1 billion years ago—twice as early as was previously thought.

Yankees win the World Series

Yankees players pile up on the pitcher's mound in celebration of their first World Series victory for 18 years.

On an impassioned night at Yankee Stadium, 56,375 fans cheered and danced as the New York Yankees beat the Atlanta Braves 3-2 to take the World Series. It was their 23rd Series victory, but the first for 18 years.

A Yankees triumph seemed improbable earlier in the week, when they lost the first two games at home, but four straight wins gave them the title.

The victory was an emotional experience, especially for Yankees' manager Joe Torre, whose brother Frank had a heart transplant on Friday. But all the Yankees felt that the win was special. Captain Darryl Strawberry said: "I can't tell you how good this feels." (→ October 29)

Cleveland, OH, Thursday 24. Boxer Mike Tyson is contesting a zoning board ruling that bans him from keeping a tiger cub on his estate. Tyson has focused on his career since assault allegations against him in April proved groundless. (→ November 10)

Shooting sets off Florida riot

The Florida city of St. Petersburg was rocked by rioting last night after a black motorist was shot dead by a white police officer. The motorist had been stopped for speeding.

The rioting began at the intersection where the shooting took place. Police were bombarded with bottles and rocks. Later the trouble worsened. Shots were fired at police cars and gasoline bombs were thrown. Firefighters were attacked when they arrived to control the fires.

Today the streets are calm. But the rioting is a brutal reminder of the continuing tension between many black residents and police in US cities. (→ November 14)

SANTA MONICA, CA, WED. 23
O.J. trial drama recommences

In a Santa Monica court today, opening statements were heard in what is effectively O.J. Simpson's second trial for the 1994 slaying of his wife, Nicole Brown Simpson, and Ronald Goldman. The victims' families have brought a civil suit against O.J., suing him for wrongful death. With the laxer rules pertaining in a civil court and a new jury, they are hoping that—this time—the outcome will be different. (→ November 22)

O.J. Simpson is back in court for a rerun of last year's "trial of the century."

Southern California, Tuesday 22. Firefighters are struggling to control wildfires that have struck the movie-star colony of Malibu. Strong winds are spreading the blaze across three counties.

MANAGUA, MONDAY 21
Sandinistas fail again in bid for power

Nicaraguan voters face complex choices.

Daniel Ortega, leader of the Sandinista National Liberation Front that ruled Nicaragua from 1979 to 1990, has failed in his bid to return to power through democratic means.

The votes in presidential elections held on Sunday are still being counted but Arnoldo Aleman, conservative ex-mayor of Managua, is already claiming victory, with a nine-point lead over Ortega. Over 80 percent of electors voted in polls that offered a choice of 25 candidates. (→ November 3)

JERUSALEM, WEDNESDAY 23
Chirac becomes a hero in Palestine after clash with Israeli security guards

French president Jacques Chirac today became the first foreign head of state to address the Palestinian Council, the parliament ruling the autonomous West Bank and Gaza.

Chirac received a rapturous welcome in the West Bank after a public clash with Israeli security guards yesterday. On a visit to the Holy Places in Jerusalem, the French president had been clearly angered by the guards who hemmed him in at every moment. At one point he shouted at their commander: "This is a provocation. Stop this now."

Although Israeli prime minister Benjamin Netanyahu apologized for the incident, it dramatized the main thrust of Chirac's visit, which was to offer France's support to Palestinian leader Yasir Arafat in his dispute with Israel. Chirac called for the creation of an independent Palestinian state and a complete withdrawal of Israel from all the occupied territories, including East Jerusalem. (→ October 29)

Young Palestinians welcome French president Jacques Chirac to Ramallah in the Palestinian-ruled West Bank.

S	M	T	W	T	F	S
		1	2	3	4	5
6	7	8	9	10	11	12
13	14	15	16	17	18	19
20	21	22	23	24	25	26
27	28	29	30	31		

Islamabad, Pakistan, 27
Life in the Pakistan capital is brought to a standstill as Islamic militants demonstrating against Prime Minister Benazir Bhutto's government clash with security forces. (→ November 4)

Kabul, Afghanistan, 27
Forces opposed to the Taleban Islamic extremists bomb Kabul for the second straight night.

Los Angeles, 28
The *Los Angeles Times* reports that a record 67,000 illegal immigrants were deported from the US from October 1995 to September 1996. This was 34 percent more deportations than in the previous 12-month period.

Luxembourg, 28
EU foreign ministers agree to prohibit European companies from complying with US legislation that penalizes firms trading with Cuba, Iran, or Libya.

Washington, DC, 29
The Democratic National Committee agrees to publish a list of campaign contributors as questions continue to be asked about contributions obtained from Indonesian and Korean businessmen by fundraiser John Huang.

West Bank, 29
Palestinians riot at the funeral of a ten-year-old Arab boy allegedly killed by a Jewish settler.

Raleigh, NC, 29
Scientists at North Carolina State University publish a study that suggests an excess of the female hormone estrogen may be partly responsible for baldness in men.

Sao Paulo, Brazil, 31
A Brazilian airliner crashes into a residential neighborhood in the city of Sao Paulo, killing at least 95 people.

London, 31
British scientists announce meteorite evidence of life on Mars that supports claims publicized by NASA in August.

Deaths
October 31. Eleanor Dulles, State Department economic expert from 1942 to 1962, in Washington, DC, at age 101.

ATLANTA, MONDAY 28

Jewell speaks about his "nightmare"

Former Olympic security guard Richard Jewell received a letter from federal prosecutors last Saturday stating that he was cleared of suspicion of involvement in the July 27 bombing at the Centennial Olympic Park. Today, Jewell spoke of his experience as a suspect in the case.

First identified as a hero for finding the knapsack containing the bomb, Jewell was then marked out by federal investigators and the media as the prime suspect. He was hounded by reporters and subjected to FBI searches and surveillance. "I lived a nightmare," Jewell said.

He has announced that he intends to sue news organizations who, he alleges, tried to pin the bombing on him. "I hope and pray that no one is ever subjected to the ordeal that I have gone through," he said.

VIENNA, TUESDAY 29

Jewish art plundered by Nazis auctioned

More than 8,000 paintings, drawings, and antiques stolen from Austrian Jews by the Nazis went up for auction in Vienna today. The proceeds will go to Holocaust survivors.

In an emotionally charged atmosphere, prices escalated well beyond the catalog guide prices. The first day of the sale netted $13 million, four times the estimate for the whole two-day auction.

The art had been stored by the Austrian authorities ever since it was recovered after World War II. They have admitted that no effort was made to locate the original owners.

The bidding in the Jewish art auction proceeded in a tense and emotional atmosphere.

New York, Tuesday 29. The New York Yankees paraded through Lower Manhattan's "Canyon of Heroes" today after winning the World Series last Saturday. According to possibly exaggerated City Hall figures, around 3.5 million people turned out to line the 1-mile route.

Million lives at risk as refugees flee battleground

Ethnic conflict in the east of Zaire, in central Africa, is threatening the lives of over a million Hutu refugees from Rwanda. A military offensive by rebel Tutsis, the Hutus' sworn enemies, has driven the refugees from their camps. Aid officials warn that, as the refugees flee, food supplies may break down and cholera erupt in their midst.

The present crisis broke out after Hutu extremists and Zairean government forces attacked Tutsis inside Zaire, trying to drive them out of areas where they have lived for more than two centuries. The Tutsis, backed by the Tutsi-dominated Rwandan government, counterattacked and routed Zairean forces. This week they took one provincial capital, Bukavu, and threatened another, Goma.

Despite their precarious condition, the Hutu refugees refuse to return to Rwanda. They fear reprisals for the massacre of 500,000 Tutsis by Hutu extremists in 1994. (→ November 13)

Rwandan Hutu refugees set up a temporary camp as they trek across eastern Zaire in search of a secure place to settle.

Tulsa, OK, Tuesday 29. Tom Lehman won the PGA Tour Championship at Southern Hills today. The victory makes him top earner on this year's Tour.

Two women rescued after 36 hours trapped under rubble

Late on Sunday, an apartment building collapsed in Heliopolis, a suburb of the Egyptian capital, Cairo. More than 150 people are believed to have been buried under the rubble.

Today, 36 hours after the disaster occurred, Samantha Miksche, 17, an Australian, and her Egyptian friend, Noha Fawzi, 19, were found alive by rescuers. They had been visiting the building with Miksche's mother to look at an apartment to rent. The mother is still missing, along with more than 100 other people.

The ruins of a Cairo apartment building that collapsed on Sunday.

Chinese dissident is jailed

After a trial lasting three hours, a Chinese court today sentenced pro-democracy activist Wang Dan to 11 years in prison for "conspiring to subvert China's government."

Wang Dan, 27, was a student leader during the Tiananmen Square protest in 1989, and he spent three years in jail after the protest was crushed. He has since continued to campaign for human rights and democracy. This is the crime for which he is punished.

Paris, Thursday 31. One of France's greatest filmmakers, Marcel Carné, died today, at age 90. His masterpiece is *Les Enfants du Paradis*, a film made during the Nazi occupation of France in World War II.

S	M	T	W	T	F	S
					1	2
3	4	5	6	7	8	9
10	11	12	13	14	15	16
17	18	19	20	21	22	23
24	25	26	27	28	29	30

Kentucky, 1
Allen Paulson, owner of champion racehorse Cigar, says the horse has run its last race. Cigar will retire to a stud farm.

London, 3
Britain's main telephone company, British Telecom, announces it plans to take over MCI Communications. It will be the largest ever foreign takeover of a US company.

Pontiac, MI, 3
Dr. Jack Kevorkian is charged with assisting in suicide and a range of other offences in connection with ten deaths.

Managua, Nicaragua, 3
Supporters of the Sandinista party protest their defeat in the recent national elections, claiming there was electoral fraud.

New Orleans, 3
Receiver Jerry Rice, playing for the San Francisco 49ers against New Orleans, becomes the first NFL player to catch 1,000 passes in his career.

Tokyo, 3
Boxer Tommy Morrison returns to the ring for the first time since being diagnosed as HIV-positive. He defeats Marcus Rhode in 1 minute and 38 seconds.

Moscow, 4
US businessman Paul Tatum is shot dead in a Moscow subway station, probably by a Russian mafia hitman.

New York, 4
Tapes of meetings of Texaco executives appear to show them using racist epithets and plotting to destroy documents relevant to a discrimination suit against the company. (→ November 14)

Bangkok, Thailand, 5
Singer Michael Jackson, on tour in Thailand, confirms that he is to have a child by 37-year-old nurse Debbie Rowe. (→ November 14)

Deaths
November 1. Junius Jayawardene, former prime minister and president of Sri Lanka, at age 90.

November 3. Jean-Bedel Bokassa, former emperor of the Central African Republic, at age 75.

REYKJAVIK, ICELAND, TUESDAY 5
Flood from glacier sweeps across Iceland

A bridge swept away by the flood that erupted from Iceland's largest glacier.

A flood expected ever since the Loki volcano erupted last month beneath Europe's largest glacier burst across Iceland today. Prime Minister David Oddsson said the flooding was happening "on a much larger scale and much faster than we expected."

The volcanic eruption stopped on October 12, but by then it had melted a mass of ice that filled a vast lake under the glacier. Today, the water broke free and sped across the plains to the ocean. Fortunately, the area in the path of the flood had been evacuated—but roads, bridges, and power lines were swept away. The damage will cost millions of dollars to repair.

ISLAMABAD, MONDAY 4
Bhutto ousted by Pakistani president

The president of Pakistan, Farook Leghari, today dismissed the country's prime minister, Benazir Bhutto, and dissolved the national assembly. Army units surrounded Ms. Bhutto's official residence and occupied television and radio stations.

Ms. Bhutto has been severely criticized for alleged corruption and her failure to cope with the country's growing financial problems.

The president promised that fresh elections would be held within three months, but some observers believe a period of military rule is a more likely outcome of the crisis.

Benazir Bhutto, ousted Pakistani leader.

New York, Sunday 3. Runners in the New York City Marathon cross the Verrazano Bridge. The men's race was won by Italian policeman Giacomo Leone.

CANNES, FRANCE, FRIDAY 8
Salinger says missile downed TWA 800

Pierre Salinger, a former White House spokesman, told an aviation conference yesterday that he had a US secret service report proving TWA Flight 800 was downed by a US Navy missile.

Ever since the crash on July 17, there have been rumors that a missile caused the disaster. The FBI says it has found "not one shred of evidence" to support the missile theory. It also emerged today that Salinger's "secret" document had been circulating on the Internet since September.

ALEXANDRIA, EGYPT, SUNDAY 3
Divers find sunken palace of Cleopatra

French marine archeologists exploring beneath the Mediterranean Sea have discovered the remains of the royal district of ancient Alexandria, where Cleopatra and Mark Antony carried on their famous love affair more than 2,000 years ago.

Frank Goddio, the leader of the archeologists, told reporters today:"It was a fantastic feeling diving on the remains of the city. To think when I touched a statue or sphinx, Cleopatra might have done the same."

The royal zone of Alexandria sank beneath the sea after an earthquake and tidal wave in AD335. It lies in the eastern harbor of modern Alexandria.

Ancient remains under the Mediterranean.

WASHINGTON, DC, WEDNESDAY 6

Clinton wins second White House term

The Clinton family savors a moment of triumph in Little Rock as the president's election victory is confirmed.

The 1996 presidential election had long looked like a one-horse race, and so it proved to be when Americans went to the polls yesterday. President Bill Clinton became the first Democrat since Franklin D. Roosevelt to win a second term.

Clinton fell just short of his goal of an absolute majority of the popular vote, taking 49 percent, as against 41 percent for Bob Dole, and 8 percent for Ross Perot. Clinton scored especially well with women, drawing 55 percent of the female vote.

It was a day of triumph for the president, but not for Democrats in general. Clinton will again face a Republican-led Congress. Indeed, in the Senate the Republican majority even increased by one seat. Notable Republican victors were Jesse Helms in North Carolina and 93-year-old Strom Thurmond in South Carolina.

The day's most depressing statistic was voter turnout. Only 49 percent of Americans voted, which was the lowest figure since 1924.

US, WEDNESDAY 6

Citizen initiatives call for change

As well as electing their representatives this week, voters across the US have also been responding to hotly contested ballot measures.

California was the site of two of the most notable results. By a substantial majority, Californians approved an initiative banning affirmative action on grounds of race or sex. They also voted to allow the medical use of marijuana. A similar initiative was approved in Arizona.

In Florida, a proposition limiting the state's ability to impose new taxes won an overwhelming majority. Voters in Colorado, however, rejected a proposal to add a new clause to the state constitution giving parents the right to "direct and control" their children's education.

Voters make their choice in Houston.

MOSCOW, TUESDAY 5

Yeltsin's heart surgery declared a success

Russian president Boris Yeltsin, age 65, today underwent seven hours of gruelling heart-bypass surgery in a Moscow hospital. The operation was more complex than expected. Yeltsin needed five heart bypasses and his heart was stopped for 68 minutes.

Tonight, Yeltsin is in intensive care and attached to an artificial respirator, but his condition is described as "stable." The US heart specialist who consulted on the operation, Michael DeBakey, said it was a total success. "President Yeltsin will be able to return to his office and carry out his duties in a normal fashion," Dr. DeBakey predicted.

President Yeltsin with Dr. Renat Akchurin, the head of the surgical team.

CAPE CANAVERAL, THURS. 7

Spacecraft blasts off for the Red Planet

A spacecraft lifted off from Cape Canaveral today on a 435-million-mile journey to Mars. The Global Surveyor should reach Mars next September. It will spend a Martian year—687 days—in orbit, studying the planet's atmosphere and climate, mapping its surface features, and providing data on its geology.

The Global Surveyor is the first of three Mars missions planned for this year, two of them American and one Russian. (→ November 18)

S	M	T	W	T	F	S
					1	2
3	4	5	6	7	8	9
10	11	12	13	14	15	16
17	18	19	20	21	22	23
24	25	26	27	28	29	30

Aberdeen, MD, 10
Fifteen noncommissioned officers are suspended at a US Army training base after allegations of sexual harassment. The case raises questions about widespread sexual abuse in the US Army.

Washington, DC, 10
ABC television journalist David Brinkley apologizes on air to President Clinton for comments he made during election-night coverage. Brinkley called Clinton "a bore" and said his election-night speech was "one of the worst I've ever heard."

Moscow, 10
Thirteen people are killed and 16 wounded when a remote-controlled bomb explodes at a cemetery. The incident, thought to be an act of Mafia vengeance, is the worst gangland killing in Russia in recent years.

Bosnia, 12
Tensions mount in the battle to unseat General Ratko Mladic, a commander in the Bosnian war, who is now wanted by the War Crimes Tribunal in The Hague. Last week Biljana Plavsic, president of the Bosnian Serb entity, announced Mladic's dismissal, but the Bosnian Serb army rallied to his support.

Oakland, MI, 13
The family of Scott Amedure is bringing a lawsuit against the *Jenny Jones Show*, as well as its owners and distributors. Amedure revealed on the *Jenny Jones Show* that he had a crush on Schmitz, who was found guilty of killing Amedure.

St. Petersburg, FL, 14
Riots erupt in this west Florida city as a white police officer is cleared of the October 24 fatal shooting of Tyron Lewis, an 18-year-old black man who had been stopped for speeding.

Deaths
November 14. Cardinal Joseph Bernardin, a senior Roman Catholic cardinal and the leader of Chicago's 2.3 million Catholics, in Chicago, at age 68.

November 15. Alger Hiss, prominent US diplomat who was accused during the Cold War of spying for Russia, in Manhattan, at age 92.

DELHI, INDIA, TUESDAY 12
Worst-ever mid-air collision kills 350 people

A Saudi Arabian Boeing 747 collided with a Kazakh Airways Ilyushin 76 about 60 miles outside the Indian capital, Delhi, today. The 312 passengers and crew on board the Boeing and the 38 people on the Ilyushin are all thought to have died, making it the world's third-worst air disaster, and the worst-ever mid-air collision.

A US Air Force cargo plane was flying into Delhi at the time. The captain described seeing "two fireballs ... diverging from each other" as the planes fell from the sky.

Burning wreckage was littered over 6 miles of farmland near the town of Charkhi Dadri. Bodies were carried away on carts as villagers aided rescue teams.

The jumbo jet was seven minutes out of New Delhi's international airport when the collision occurred. The incoming Kazakh flight was supposed to be flying 1,000 ft above the jumbo. The Indian government has ordered a full inquiry.

The remains of the Ilyushin 76 that collided with a jumbo jet near Delhi.

AUSTRALIA, THURSDAY 14
Jackson weds for second time

Michael Jackson in Sydney last week.

Pop superstar Michael Jackson today wed Debbie Rowe, a 37-year-old nurse who is carrying his child. "Please respect our privacy and let us enjoy this exciting time," Jackson said in a written statement. The couple has known each other for 15 years, and it was announced last week that Rowe will give birth to the singer's child early in 1997. In 1994, Jackson wed Lisa Marie Presley, but that marriage collapsed earlier this year, with Presley citing "irreconcilable differences."

WASHINGTON, DC, MONDAY 11
Bowles is new chief of staff

Deputy chief of staff Harold Ickes announced today that he is quitting the White House. This follows the appointment last week of Erskine Bowles, millionaire southern banker, as the chief of staff for President Clinton's second term. Bowles, 51, replaces Leon Panetta.

Bowles has been preferred over the Democrat Ickes as part of the president's drive to steer his administration toward the "vital center."

US, Monday 11. The holiday movie season kicks off with Disney's *Ransom*, directed by Ron Howard. It stars Oscar-winner Mel Gibson as a tycoon who attempts to turn the tables on his son's kidnappers.

GOMA, ZAIRE, WEDNESDAY 13

Multinational force planned to avert Zaire tragedy

A multinational force is being organized to fly into eastern Zaire. The aim of the force will be to protect relief supplies for a million refugees threatened by starvation. Fighting between Tutsi rebels and Hutu militias is disrupting food aid.

The US has agreed to join the multinational force, which will be commanded by a Canadian officer, Lieutenant General Maurice Baril. Other countries that have promised to take part include Britain, France, Italy, Spain, and South Africa.

The situation in eastern Zaire has led to severe doubts about the relief mission, however. There are fears that the multinational force might find itself caught up in the Zairean conflict. The US has made it a condition of its participation that a cease-fire must first be agreed between Tutsi and Hutu fighters around the rebel-held town of Goma, through which relief supplies are to be channeled. (→ November 18)

A young Hutu refugee in eastern Zaire, an area torn apart by ethnic conflict and the aftermath of genocidal massacres.

Los Angeles, Sunday 10. Singer Frank Sinatra, 80, left the hospital yesterday, despite reports that he is close to death. Sinatra was admitted to the hospital for treatment on a pinched nerve.

NEW YORK, THURSDAY 14

Texaco settles racism lawsuit for $176 million

The oil company Texaco today agreed to pay out $176.1 million to settle a racial discrimination lawsuit brought on behalf of 1,400 black employees. The plaintiffs, who were seeking up to $520 million, charged that the oil company denied blacks promotion and discriminated against them. Part of their case was a tape recording of two Texaco executives who appeared to make racist remarks. Black organizations have called for a boycott of Texaco gas stations and for investors to drop Texaco stock. (→ November 20)

Las Vegas, Sunday 10. In one of the greatest-ever upsets in boxing, Evander Holyfield defeated Mike Tyson by a technical knockout in the eleventh round last night. Holyfield, an 11-1 underdog, now holds the World Boxing Association heavyweight title.

WASHINGTON, DC, FRIDAY 15

Cancer rates reported falling in US

According to two new studies, the number of cancer deaths in the US has declined for the first time since statistics began to be kept early this century.

Separate studies by the University of Alabama at Birmingham and the National Cancer Institute show that cancer rates have fallen by 2.6 percent since 1991. This reverses a trend in which the rates rose every decade, reaching a peak in 1990. Experts say that the decline is most likely due to reduced smoking and better treatment and prevention methods.

November

Western Australia, 17
Australian yachtsman David Dicks, 18, sails into Fremantle to become the youngest person to complete a nonstop cirumnavigation of the world.

Calais, France, 18
A major fire breaks out on a freight train in the Channel Tunnel that links England and France. The tunnel is closed for repair.

Washington, DC, 18
The CIA announces that one of its senior officers, Harold Nicholson, has been arrested for spying for the Russians.

Vatican, 19
During a meeting with Fidel Castro in the Vatican, Pope John Paul II accepts an invitation to visit Cuba next year.

Jerusalem, 19
Four Israeli soldiers, convicted of negligently shooting dead an 18-year-old Palestinian, are fined one agora, equivalent to a third of a US cent.

Quincy, IL, 19
A United Express commuter plane collides with a private plane at a runway intersection. Fourteen people die.

Chicago, 19
Albert Belle becomes the highest-paid player in baseball, joining the Chicago White Sox with a five-year contract worth $52.5 million.

Washington, DC, 20
Republican members of the House of Representatives vote to keep Newt Gingrich as speaker of the House.

Los Angeles, 20
Pamela Anderson, a star of the popular TV series *Baywatch*, is suing for divorce from rock drummer Tommy Lee. They have a five-month-old son.

Hobart, Tasmania, 21
Martin Bryant is sentenced to life imprisonment for shooting 35 people dead at Port Arthur in April.

Hong Kong, 21
Thirty-nine people are killed and 80 injured in a fire in a high-rise office building. It is Hong Kong's worst fire disaster for 40 years.

Moroni, Comoros, 23
An Ethiopian Airlines Boeing 767, hijacked between Addis Ababa and Nairobi, runs out of fuel off the Comoro islands and crashes into the Indian Ocean. At least 123 people are killed.

Sydney, Thursday 21. After a sensational performance on his first US PGA tour, 20-year-old golfer Tiger Woods plays in the Australian Open today.

BUCHAREST, MONDAY 18

Election ends communist rule in Romania

Emil Constantinescu, victorious leader of the Romanian Democratic Convention.

Seven years after a revolution overthrew Romania's communist dictator, Nicolae Ceausescu, the grip of former communists on the country has at last been shaken off. In the second round of elections held yesterday, President Ion Iliescu, a top communist official under Ceausescu who has held power ever since the revolution, was defeated by a democratic opposition candidate, Emil Constantinescu.

Constantinescu led an alliance of anticommunist opposition groups. He called the result "a victory for millions of Romanians who lived through years of repression."

SANTA MONICA, CA, FRIDAY 22

O.J. Simpson takes the witness stand at last

More than a year after being found not guilty in the "trial of the century," O.J. Simpson today took the witness stand for the first time to answer questions about the murders of his ex-wife, Nicole Brown Simpson, and Ronald Goldman.

Questioned by Daniel Petrocelli, the attorney for Ronald Goldman's father, Simpson denied slapping or punching Nicole, despite being confronted with photographs showing her bruised and scratched. He said Nicole lied about him hitting her.

During last year's trial, Simpson exercised his right not to testify. But now, facing a wrongful death lawsuit in a civil court, he has had to take the stand or lose the suit by default.

The case is largely a rerun of the evidence presented in the murder trial, although judge Hiroshi Fujisaki has ruled out testimony about racist attitudes in the LAPD. New evidence includes a photo allegedly showing Simpson wearing Bruno Magli shoes of the kind that left bloody footprints at the scene of the crime.

Bangalore, Tuesday 19. Hindus are protesting the decision to hold this year's Miss World pageant in Bangalore, India, on Saturday. Today, an Indian court turned down an application to ban the pageant. Extremists have threatened to commit suicide at the event.

New York, Monday 18. British actor Daniel Day-Lewis (above) has married Rebecca Miller, daughter of playwright Arthur Miller, it was announced today.

NEW YORK, TUESDAY 19

US stands alone in vetoing reelection of UN leader

At a meeting of the UN Security Council today, US representative, Madeleine Albright, vetoed a second four-year term for the current UN secretary-general, Boutros Boutros Ghali. All other 14 council members supported Boutros Ghali's reelection.

The US veto can be overruled by the UN General Assembly, but this is unlikely to happen. The UN desperately needs $1.4 billion, which it is owed by the US. If the US does not get its way, it is unlikely ever to pay up.

UN Secretary-General Boutros Boutros Ghali, hoping for a second term in office.

ZAIRE, MONDAY 18

Refugees stream home to Rwanda

Hundreds of thousands of Hutu refugees set off for Rwanda from Mugunga camp, in Zaire.

MOSCOW, MONDAY 18

Russian Mars probe lands in Pacific

Russia's space program is in disarray today after the Mars-96 spacecraft, launched from a site in Kazakhstan on Saturday, fell back to Earth and crashed into the Pacific Ocean.

Experts are still analyzing the cause of the failure, but it appears that booster rockets, which should have propelled the craft deep into space, failed to fire.

More fundamentally, the setback is blamed on severe underfunding of the Russian space program since the break up of the Soviet Union.

As advance parties of troops from a planned multinational relief force arrived in central Africa at the end of last week, the Hutu refugees they had come to save from starvation began to leave their camps in Zaire and return to Rwanda. Today, a column of refugees 50 miles long is filling the road from Goma in Zaire eastward to the Rwandan border. An estimated 400,000 refugees have crossed the border since last Friday.

The sudden abandonment of the refugee camps follows a rout of Hutu militias by Tutsi rebel forces backed by the Rwandan government. The surviving Hutu militiamen have fled, apparently intending to regroup in the Zairean interior. Freed from coercion by the militia, the majority of Hutus seemed eager to go home. Refugees interviewed by the press seemed confident they would not face retribution for the Hutu massacre of Tutsis in Rwanda in 1994, the starting point of the current crisis.

It seems certain that the deployment of the multinational force will now not go ahead as originally conceived. Observers on the ground in Zaire are warning, however, that the refugee problem is far from resolved. The future of about half a million refugees remains in doubt, and the prospect of further fighting in the zone remains a potent threat to the humanitarian aid effort.

US, Sunday 17. Still near the top of the box office charts a month after opening, the film of Lorenzo Carcaterra's bestseller *Sleepers* stars Brad Pitt (above center) and Robert De Niro.

Index

110

Picture credits

The position of the illustrations is indicated by letters: b=bottom, l=left, m=middle, r=right, t=top.